S0-BSF-089

WHATEVER BECAME OF . . . ?

Third Series

Also by the Author

Whatever Became Of...? First Series
Whatever Became Of...? Second Series

WHATEVER BECAME OF . . . ?

Third Series

by
RICHARD LAMPARSKI

CROWN PUBLISHERS, INC., NEW YORK

Acknowledgments

The author would like to express thanks to the following people who helped in the preparation of this book: Clifford May, Peter Hanson, John Robbins, Jon Virzi, Joe Riccuiti, Don Koll, Danny Frank, Michael Knowles (a colleague), Kirk Crivello, Marvin Paige, Jim Britain, Charles Higham, and Clayton Cole; and A.F.T.R.A., *Movie Star News,* and Cinemabilia for their cooperation.

The photographs contained in this book are from the author's own collection, or were kindly supplied by the personalities themselves, or are part of the collections of Jon Virzi, John Robbins, Diana Keyt, and Clifford May.

Individuals whose names carry an asterisk (*) in the text appear as separate segments in Volume One of *Whatever Became of . . . ?* Those with a double asterisk (**) appear as separate segments in *Whatever Became of . . . ? Second Series.*

Fifth Printing, August, 1974

© 1970 BY RICHARD LAMPARSKI

LIBRARY OF CONGRESS CATALOG CARD NUMBER: 76–127506

All rights reserved. No part of this book may be reproduced or utilized in any form or by any means, electronic or mechanical, including photocopying, recording, or by any information storage and retrieval system, without permission in writing from the Publisher. Inquiries should be addressed to Crown Publishers, Inc., 419 Park Avenue South, New York, N.Y. 10016

PRINTED IN THE UNITED STATES OF AMERICA

Published simultaneously in Canada by General Publishing Company Limited

*To Amaryllis Beirne-Keyt, born May 26, 1970, with
hope for a better world through peace and
social justice for all her generation*

CONTENTS

In Alphabetical Order

6

July 1954 when it was still politically safe for Nixon to be
seen with him. *UPI*

SHERMAN ADAMS

The central figure in the scandal that rocked the Eisenhower administration was born Llewellyn Sherman Adams in the village of East Dover, Vermont, on January 8, 1899. Shortly after his birth, his father, a grocer,
moved the family to Providence, Rhode Island, where he attended high
school. During World War I he served in the Marine Corps, and in 1920 he
received a B.A. degree from Dartmouth College.

Adams entered business as a lumberjack with the Black River Lumber
Company in southern Vermont, advancing shortly to logging foreman and
then company treasurer. When he left the firm to enter politics in 1940, he
was president. As a member of the New Hampshire House of Representatives, Adams supported Thomas E. Dewey ** at the G.O.P. Convention of
1944. That same year he was elected to the United States House of Representatives. Although he quickly aligned himself with the "Young Republicans" of Congress, his record shows him to be not a liberal but a moderate
conservative. After being defeated for the gubernatorial nomination in
1946, he tried again and won the 1948 primary and election. He was reelected in 1950.

In 1951 Adams was one of six Republican governors who called for the
nomination of General Eisenhower, and he was largely responsible for the
defeat of Taft in the crucial New Hampshire primary of 1952. After Ike's
nomination in Chicago that summer, Adams was chosen by the nominee as
his chief of staff for the campaign.

When Eisenhower entered the White House, Sherman Adams went with
him as presidential assistant. Such was his influence over the president that
many referred to him as "the shadow president." Adams had final say over
patronage and appointments. His curt, negative replies to requests for fa-
vors, appointments, and information earned him the title the Abominable
No-Man along with the enmity of some high-ranking Republicans.

As the typical New Englander, with his taciturn manner and frugal habits, Adams was a choice target for scandal. On June 12, 1958, it was dis-

closed that he had intervened with government agencies on several occasions on behalf of his long-time friend, Bernard Goldfine, a Boston millionaire. It was also learned that this public servant with the puritanical pose had accepted a vicuña overcoat, a twenty-four-hundred-dollar oriental rug and that his hotel bills exceeding two thousand dollars had been paid by Goldfine. At first the president stood firmly behind him and explained his loyalty in his refusal to fire him: "Because I need him." But as Goldfine's unorthodox business transactions made the front pages day after day and the elections of that year neared, Adams's position became impossible, and on September 22, 1958, he went before television cameras to announce that he was resigning as a result of "the campaign of vilification" against him. Eisenhower never reprimanded Adams except to say that he felt his assistant had "erred in judgment."

In defense of accusations about his own finances, part of Nixon's campaign oratory of 1952 was his jibes at Democratic corruption—he referred to his wife's "good Republican cloth coat." In the elections of 1958, the Democrats swept into office in the biggest landslide since the New Deal with jokes about the vice-president's old friend's vicuña coat, and the Nixon-Adams friendship, both political and social, had ended abruptly when his indiscretions were made public.

After leaving public life, Adams spoke before gatherings of businessmen in New England and lectured on political history at Wooster College and the University of New Hampshire. Neither before audiences nor in his 1961 book *First-Hand Report* did he ever add any more information to the record of his extra-curricular activities during his White House years.

Bernard Goldfine died in 1967 after declaring bankruptcy, but his one-time friend lives quietly with his wife, Rachel, in Lincoln, New Hampshire, where he has developed a highly successful ski resort on Loon Mountain. Adams has nothing to do with local politics and never discusses his past, even with close friends.

If the image of the Eisenhower administration had been less self-righteous or Adams's personality less abrasive to those on Capitol Hill, the whole thing might have been no more than a little embarrassing for everyone. With typical Washington cynicism one politician said recently of the whole affair: "Poor Sherman didn't do anything most people here don't do every day. He just got caught."

The former presidential assistant on the trails at his $1.5 million resort in the White Mountains. *UPI*

At the time of her first arrest
Yokohama, Japan, 1945. *UPI*

TOKYO ROSE

The woman accused of broadcasting propaganda from Japan during World
War II was born Iva Ikuko Toguri d'Aquino in Los Angeles on July 4, 1916.
In early 1941, after obtaining a degree in zoology from UCLA, she left her
Japanese-American parents to visit a sick aunt in Japan, as well as to study
the language. It was after Pearl Harbor when she tried to return to her
homeland, and she was told by the Japanese authorities that nisei would
not be repatriated. She was advised to get a job since she no longer could
communicate with her family and had no source of income.

Iva had taken stenography for a short time in the States and now was
given a position as a typist at Radio Japan. Since she knew very few people
and practically no Japanese, she became friendly with a group of prisoners
of war who were doing a program called *Zero Hour*. They asked her to fill
a fifteen-minute slot in the hour show playing American records. Her billing
was "Orphan Ann." Iva says she did nothing more than make light chatter
about how wonderful it would be when they could all return home. It was
stressed that she, too, was an American by birth. "The Japs had no idea of
psychological warfare," she says. "Our programs were thoroughly innocuous.
How could I betray my country? No one who had lived in both countries
could believe that a tiny island could defeat the United States."

At the war's end she was held for a time by the United States Army. Then
Walter Winchell announced on his Sunday night radio program that
"Tokyo Rose," the name the GIs had given her, was free, and quoted from
an emotional letter written to him by a Gold Star Mother. Immediately
after, Iva was arrested and held incommunicado for one year, one month,
and one day. During her three-month trial it was shown that several women
had broadcast regularly from Japan but no others were indicted. Neither
was anyone else associated with her radio program brought to trial.

Fortunately for her, five recordings of her broadcasts, which were obtained from a Silver Springs, Maryland, collector who had recorded them as
they came over short wave, proved worthless to the prosecution. However,

Iva could not afford to bring in vital witnesses to corroborate her testimony, whereas the federal government spared no expense. Of the eight counts brought against her, she was convicted on one only: a reported broadcast for which no record of any kind had been produced. The jury foreman told Iva afterward how sorry he was about the verdict.

Iva spent six years in the West Virginia federal prison for women where she met a fellow inmate, Axis Sally,** on several brief occasions.

Iva is legally separated from d'Aquino, her Portuguese husband, whom she met in Japan. She will not discuss him except to say she does not know his whereabouts. She is a convert to Roman Catholicism but has not practiced her religion for years.

She goes unnoticed as the manageress of a small notions store in Chicago's Japanese section, on Clark Street. She also runs her father's importing business. Together they sponsor Japanese students who wish to study in the United States.

In reflecting on her past, Iva refers to the thousands of Japanese, Americans, and foreign born who had their property and freedom taken from them when they were interned in the United States during the war. "Guess who recommended that they be picked up?" she asks. "Guess who, as attorney general of California, signed the order? That great friend of the down-trodden, Chief Justice Earl Warren!"

Along with all those whose belongings were impounded and confiscated, Iva's father was awarded ten cents on the prewar dollar for his losses. When the Supreme Court made its judgment, Justice Warren abstained. As for Iva, her lawyers, who had never accepted a cent for her defense or appeals, are petitioning President Nixon for her full pardon. Iva does not take kindly to interviewers, and when asked to pose for a photograph, she at first hesitated, then cracked: "Oh, what difference does it make? Americans think we all look alike anyway!"

Tokyo Rose today, in her Chicago apartment. *Diane Arbus*

PETER TOWNSEND

Princess Margaret Rose's star-crossed lover was born in Rangoon on November 22, 1914. Townsend's father was a lieutenant colonel in the British Army. The boy's education at good English public schools and finally at Haileybury College was a considerable financial strain on the family, but he was an excellent student. Following the military tradition of his ancestors, Peter entered the service with the intention of becoming a career officer. His father was somewhat upset that his son chose the Royal Air Force but he made such a good record in such a short time as a flier that all was soon forgiven.

Peter led the first mission to shoot down an enemy plane over English soil. During the war he became a hero in the Battle of Britain, commanding a squadron of fighter planes. He was shot down once over the North Sea in 1940 and another time had to have a toe amputated after an air fight.

When he was twenty-nine years old, Townsend was transferred to London, where he became equerry of George VI, the first commoner in history to be so honored. It was at his first interview with the king that Peter was to meet briefly the thirteen-year-old Princess Margaret Rose.

By 1950 the dashing Townsend was a known intimate of the royal family, although it was some time before the public became aware of just how intimate he was with one of the king's daughters. The first hint that he was anything more than a charming escort came in 1952 when he and his wife, a brigadier's daughter he had married in July of 1941, filed for divorce. Perhaps to squelch rumors that were brewing in London, the Queen Mother announced in 1953 that Peter would henceforth be her equerry.

Actually, the foreign press had been reporting the romance for some time before it became known in English papers. Through 1954 and 1955 it was the big question for anyone who takes such people seriously. Would she renounce her right to succession and marry the divorced commoner? One London paper ran the classic headline: "Margaret to Choose Between Peter and Spinsterhood."

For a while it seemed that the British establishment was clearing the way for the union, but then, on October 31, 1955, the princess announced to the world that she had decided not to marry Group Captain Peter Townsend. Queen Elizabeth sent Peter to Brussels as the British air attaché. When he resigned his commission and left the post in 1956, he told the press that he would never return to England. Never. He has since returned many times. In fact, he has since met with Margaret Rose on several occasions.

Townsend, who had practically no money of his own, embarked on a well-publicized world tour from which a documentry film was made. It, like his several books, was no great success. In 1959 he married the daughter of a wealthy Belgian cigarette manufacturer who took a dim view of his poor, non-Catholic son-in-law. His wife had been a photographer on his tour.

12

For a while the couple lived in the United States, in Connecticut, although Peter had once described the United States as a country of traveling salesmen. Also, they lived for short periods in London, practically next door to his former wife and their two sons, Giles and Hugo, and in Paris, where they claimed their privacy was invaded by neighbors with binoculars.

The Townsends now live in a large old country house in the tiny hamlet of Lévis Saint Nom, twenty-five miles outside Paris on the edge of the Marly forest. They have three children: Marie-Isabelle, Marie-Françoise, and Pierre. This time it was their neighbors who complained about *them*. They were riding across private property and ruining crops. Not included in the official complaint to the mayor was the local resentment of Peter's snobbishness. His ideas on social distinction have been called positively medieval.

Townsend has been involved professionally in the past few years as a public relations consultant and spokesman for wine industries, both French and American. For a time he was a member of the Board of the Gold Seal Vineyards and has been given the title director of European operations for the famed Maxim's restaurant. Townsend fancies himself a great connoisseur and gourmet.

His last brush with publicity came in 1969, when he made a tour in behalf of the film *The Battle of Britain*. He served as technical adviser during the filming while Antony Armstrong-Jones, Margaret Rose's husband, acted as still photographer. They studiously avoided each other. Although he becomes annoyed when anyone asks him about the crisis that his affair with the princess brought about, the questions are not sufficiently provoking to make him avoid the press. If he doesn't miss the spotlight it is because he is never long out of it.

During one interview recently, the war hero startled a few of his fellow veterans when he explained his feelings toward national conflict: "If presidents, generals or kings want to fight—let them. But please leave the rest of us alone!"

At the height of his notoriety, 1955, en route to a private racetrack in France. *UPI*

Margaret Rose's spurned lover still makes news. *New York Daily News*

Announcing the failure of the London Conference with the Soviet Union, 1945. *CBS Radio*

JAMES F. BYRNES

President Truman's secretary of state was born in 1879 in a "little sagging-galleried house" in Charleston, South Carolina. His father had died before James was born, leaving his mother penniless. She supported her children with the income from a dress shop, but James had to leave school when he was fourteen years old to help out. His first job was as an office boy in a law firm. Seven years later he was working in Aiken, South Carolina, as a court reporter and studying law under a judge. He was admitted to the bar in 1903. In 1908 James purchased the *Aiken Journal and Review,* and became its editor.

Byrnes first ran for election in 1908, when he won the post of solicitor of the Second South Carolina Circuit. The post, which was the equivalent of district attorney, gave him the authority to mount a thorough cleanup of Barnwell County.

Two years later, in his first congressional election campaign, he commented: "I run with nothing but gall." Gall won with a fifty-seven-vote majority. During his early years he was accused of jeopardizing white supremacy in his area by supporting a constitutional amendment for direct senatorial primaries.

He forced formation of the House Committee on Roads from which grew the present federal road-aid system. He frankly admitted that his interests were highly pragmatic when he explained, "We fellows in Congress mostly have got to promise our people something from the Treasury and in the old days in the South and West we generally promised them federal roads."

He tried for the Senate in 1924 but was defeated. In 1930 he made another attempt, this one successful, and served until 1941. In 1936 he managed the Relief Bill that provided $4.8 billion in relief funds for those who were hit hardest by the depression. Shortly after its passage and application he stated that he regretted his part as he was "disillusioned by its results." In 1938 he had worked hard to defeat labor's Wage-Hour Bill, which the unions had been promoting as a real break for the working man. The next year he attempted to reduce the appropriations for the WPA, the employer of hundreds of thousands of depression victims.

In 1940 Byrnes had his heart set on the vice-presidential spot on the Democratic ticket but lost out to Henry Wallace. His close friend Franklin D. Roosevelt appointed him in 1941 to a seat on the United States Supreme Court, but he left that post in 1942 to become the director of Economic Stabilization. Then he became director of the Office of War Mobilization in 1943 and head of the new Office of War Mobilization and Reconversion from 1944 to 1945.

In 1944 Byrnes had again made a valiant effort to secure the second spot on FDR's ticket but Truman was picked instead. He has always blamed the labor unions, though as a consistent antilaborite during his terms in Congress it should have come as no surprise. Working conditions and wages among his constituency were always among the worst in the country. However, there were no hard feelings between him and Harry Truman, who named him secretary of state in June, 1945. Unfortunately Brynes's reactionary politics and lack of vision at his meetings with the Soviets in Moscow, Potsdam, and Paris did nothing to avert the cold war. He resigned in 1947, citing poor health as the reason. *Speaking Frankly,* his reminiscenses of his State Department years, was published that year and his autobiography, *All in One Lifetime,* was brought out in 1958.

Brynes's last public post was governor of South Carolina from 1951 to 1955. During those years he was very vocal on states' rights and segregation. He was a strong champion of both, and still is. Black civil rights leaders could only feel their worst suspicions of President Nixon were true when he paid a forty-five-minute call on the elder statesman on his ninetieth birthday. On that occasion, Nixon said of him, "Never in American history has one man held more high offices with more distinction," and the band then played "Dixie." This is the man who opposes school integration because of his "instinctive desire for the preservation of our races." He has said, "It is useless to argue whether the racial instinct is right or wrong. It exists."

He and his wife of sixty-four years live in a one-and-a-half-story white brick Colonial house on a tree-shaded street in Columbia, South Carolina. His public appearances have been limited greatly by a stroke and subsequent minor surgery suffered a couple of years ago.

President and Mrs. Nixon help Byrnes and his wife celebrate his combination ninetieth birthday and sixty-third wedding anniversary in South Carolina. *UPI*

Left to right: Maxine, Patti, and La Verne Andrews in a 1941 publicity photo.

THE ANDREWS SISTERS

The world-famous musical trio were born in Minneapolis, Minnesota, to a Greek restaurant owner and his Norwegian-born wife. There were La Verne, 1915, Maxine, 1917, and Patti, 1920. When Patti was only six years old they all began singing together at amateur nights in local theatres and on radio stations. Mr. Andrews disapproved but their mother encouraged the girls so that they would have a mutual interest and would cease their quarreling. They would race home from school each day to hear the Boswell Sisters * sing on Bing Crosby's radio program. "Music is the one thing we had in common. We never agreed on hair styles or clothes but we were always together when he chose material and arrangements," said Maxine recently, who acknowledges that she was the rebel of the family.

After "starving for seven years" with such bands as Leon Belasco and Larry Rich, the girls sang one night in 1937 on a radio broadcast from the Hotel Edison in New York. When Dave Kapp heard them on a cab radio he set up a recording session for them at Decca Records, which was run by his brother Jack. They cut "Nice Work If You Can Get It" as the hit side backed by "Bei Mir Bist du Schoen." It was the second side that took off and sold over a million copies. For that effort they were paid the flat sum of fifty dollars, with no royalties. Thereafter Decca gave them a new contract that paid them a five-cent royalty on every record sold, something that only Bing Crosby had been able to command until then. A few of the hits that followed were "The Hut Sut Song," "Three Little Fishes," "Rum and Coca-Cola," "Apple Blossom Time," and "Beer Barrel Polka."

Although they never matched their idols, the Boswells, for perfect rhythm and harmony, the Andrewses became much more famous and made far more money. Maxine's husband, Lou Levy, was their manager and saw to it that the girls had the best arrangers in the business as well as the first pick of new material. No one did more to swing the sound of the late thirties and forties than these three girls, who never learned to read music.

Although they were unhappy with all of their movie appearances, they couldn't complain about the huge fees they collected for them. A few are *Argentine Nights* (1940), *In the Navy* (1941), *What's Cookin'?* (1942), *Follow the Boys* (1944), and *The Road to Rio* (1947). In a number of films they worked with Bing Crosby, as they did on records and on his radio program.

In 1948 their mother died, followed shortly by their father, and in 1950 Maxine and Lou Levy were divorced. "Everything seemed to catch up with us at once," said Maxine. In 1954, Patti filed suit over her mother's estate, and by this time the girls had agreed to go their separate ways. They were reunited a few times but it was never the same. They began wearing different clothes and coiffures in their club act in Vegas and elsewhere during the sixties. But it was their vastly different temperaments that caused the real clashes.

The break was permanent in 1967. La Verne died of cancer. Patti, who never left show business, is available as a singer and comedienne. In 1970 she made a guest appearance on the Lucille Ball television show and had a cameo part in the movie *Phynx* (1970). She and her pianist-conductor husband, Walter Weschler, have been married nineteen years but have no children. They live with their two dogs in Encino, California. Patti and Maxine often speak on the phone but do not see each other very much anymore. When they do, they never discuss their professional interests. Maxine was for two years beginning in 1968 dean of women at Paradise College in Lake Tahoe, California. After teaching speech and drama there she became interested in group therapy and has formed a foundation to work with drug addicts and delinquents, using the encounter method. Of her own life, she says: "I always felt oppressed except when I was singing. Now I don't sing and I never feel anything but free. My kids, Aleda and Peter, and I have gone through a lot together, and now I can say that we're really friends. I don't miss the act for one minute. I no longer need it. I'm free."

Maxine in her office above Hollywood's Sunset Strip. *Clifford May*

Patti, a singer-comedienne now. *Warner Bros.—7 Arts*

Giving the Communist salute at the 1936 party convention. *UPI*

EARL BROWDER

America's former "Head Red" was born in Wichita, Kansas, in 1891. He was one of ten children and at the age of ten had to leave school to go to work because his father became ill. It was the end of his formal education, with the exception of a mail-order law course. Earl held such jobs as telegraph delivery boy and ledger clerk at weekly salaries ranging from $1.50 to $3.50. His conversion to Unitarianism from his original Methodist faith, and then to populism, socialism, and communism, derived more from humanitarian instincts than bitterness over his jobs. He admits that he was relatively well treated by his bosses, although they strongly objected to his political leanings. His last position was as a $16-per-week bookkeeper, at age twenty-one.

When America entered World War I, Earl and his brother William, a close associate until his death, filed suit to stop the governor of Kansas from executing the draft laws. Subsequently the Browder brothers were indicted for refusing to register and conspiring to block the draft, and were sentenced to three years in prison. During his imprisonment Earl read a great deal and continued his studies of Karl Marx's teachings, which he had begun even before the Russian Revolution. It was during his time in Leavenworth Prison that he made friends with his boyhood hero, "Big Bill" Haywood, a giant in the labor movement.

After his release in 1920, Earl Browder joined the Communist party, which operated clandestinely because of the considerable "Red Scare" at the time. Earlier he had met William Z. Foster when the two were in the Syndicalist League of North America, and Earl edited their magazine, *The Toiler*. Now Foster was a top Communist party official and Browder soon became his man Friday. In 1921, the time of the great famine, Browder visited Russia as a member of the Trade Union Congress, and during the twenties made several lengthy trips to China, where he became friends with Chou En-lai. He returned from the Orient only a few days before Wall Street's Black Tuesday, October 29, 1929.

In 1930 Foster was very ill and Earl Browder took over as general secretary of the Communist party. It was thought then that he was favored by Stalin as being easily controlled from the Kremlin, but, whatever the reason, Browder and Stalin never did any more than shake hands. "I took a good long look at Joe Stalin and figured him a good man to stay away from," he said. It was also rumored that Browder and President Roosevelt were friendlier than they would have liked known, but Browder claims never to have met or spoken with FDR. He ran against Roosevelt on the Communist ticket in 1936 and 1940 but admits that he did so only in the hope of helping FDR's reelection by splitting the vote against him. During FDR's second term Browder had supported Stalin in the Stalin-Trotsky debates. "If Trotsky had won, it would have been a disaster for the world. He was the same as the Chinese today. Revolution to him was a religion," says Browder today.

During his sixteen years as the head of the United States Communist party, membership increased greatly. Although he personally opposed it as impractical, the party was the first to propose self-determination for black Americans. Two of his schemes were unemployment insurance, which he suggested as early as 1933, and strong civil rights legislation.

In 1946 Browder's tenure ended abruptly when it was decided that he was too firmly committed to American-Soviet friendship. Thereafter he became a Soviet publishers' representative, a job he owed to his old friend Molotov.

Browder claims he was always firmly committed to communism in the United States but under a democratic constitution, and that it could have come about through the ballot box. Of those who still remember him, he says, "A lot of people still hate me, and not all of them are on the Right. Old political feuds die hard." He considers himself "left of center" at present and is a bitter critic of the Soviet Union's intervention in Hungary and Czechoslovakia.

Whatever Earl Browder's motivations were, he was certainly not in it for the money. In the late thirties, at the crest of his career, his reported salary was thirty-five dollars a week. He has never owned a car, a house, or land. Until the death of his wife some years ago, he resided in Yonkers, a generally unfashionable section of New York. Since 1964 he has lived in Princeton, New Jersey, with one of his three sons, all mathematics instructors at different universities. Browder describes them as "liberal Democrats." Once a week Earl comes into Manhattan for dinner with some of his old comrades. His sole source of income is Social Security.

The aged Marxist following an interview by Clifford May, a Sarah Lawrence student leader. *Diana Keyt*

In the fifties, still America's number one interviewer. *NBC Radio*

MARY MARGARET McBRIDE

The First Lady of Radio was born into a farming family in Paris, Missouri, in 1899. She grew up there and in 1919 received a B.A. from the University of Missouri, subsequently taking a job as a reporter with the Cleveland *Press* after a stint with a local paper. Newspaperwomen were rare but Mary Margaret made good quickly with her unusual angles to her stories and an uncanny ability at interviews. Soon she was writing feature stories for national magazines, until the depression hit her hard, especially since her parents relied on her for their support. When in 1934 she had a call to go over to WOR, a Manhattan radio station, she thought it slightly ridiculous. Her voice is hardly the kind used on radio, then or now. It is a homey voice with a heavy midwestern twang that has been called "folksy," and is as free of pretension as Mary Margaret herself. Three times she auditioned for the producer. When finally she was hired, at twenty-five dollars a week, they told her she would broadcast under the name Martha Deane. The plan was for her to create the character of a grandmother, with many grandchildren, and to make constant reference to them during her talks and interviews. After under three weeks broadcasting in the character of the grandmother, in the middle of a description of the cute antics of a grandchild, she got confused, forgot the child's name, and blurted out that she was not Martha Deane, not a grandmother, that in fact she wasn't even married. The audience loved the frankness and she continued for some time. But the style she had developed during these years at WOR would never change. She always insisted on doing commercials her way and was adamant about not accepting a product on her show unless she had used it herself, and liked it. She had a waiting list of prospective, patient, sponsors just hanging around until the greatest personal saleswoman in radio would get around to pitching their products.

In 1937 Mary Margaret moved to CBS, in 1941 to NBC, and in 1950 to ABC. One of her show's many distinctive features was that she insisted on her guest's first interview or none at all. This never was an official policy but word got around in the trade quickly and no author, politician, movie star, inventor, etc. was foolish enough to miss a chance to be interviewed by the queen of them all. Her audience was on a much higher intellectual level than that of the soap operas, and she never talked down to her audience or guests. The genius of her interviewing skill lay in the fact that she is a good listener, and unlike then—or now—a guest was allowed to talk. While there was a naïve quality to her voice, her questions were pointed and well thought out. People divulged things to her on the air that they had never told their spouses or lawyers.

For her fifth anniversary on the air, fans packed the Grand Central Palace, for her tenth, Madison Square Garden, and five years later they nearly filled Yankee Stadium. A rose was named for her, Fred Allen joked about her, and Bob and Ray parodied her. She was named, along with Mrs. Roosevelt, Sister Kenny, Emily Post, and Dorothy Thompson, as one of America's five most important women.

In 1954 her close friend and manager, Stella Karns, died of cancer. Miss McBride gave up her six-day-a-week, sixty-minute radio program and tried television briefly, and then retired her show. For a while she made guest appearances with Tex and Jinx McCrary. She appeared also with Jack Paar and Mike Wallace but throughout the late fifties she was spending more and more time at home in the Catskills. Her book *A Long Way from Missouri* was published in 1959, followed in 1960 by *Out of the Air,* recounting the years of "the most radio-active woman in America." She made the rounds of the interview shows to plug it and then retired to West Shokan, New York. Mary Margaret lives alone in a reconverted barn ("but it's not precious at all!") with a beautiful view of a reservoir and the mountains. But she is still in radio, doing a thrice-weekly show, *Your Hudson Valley Neighbor,* over a local station, wearing one of the many Chinese kimonos that were her trademark through the years. A couple of years ago when Peter Lind Hayes and Mary Healy took a vacation from their morning WOR show, Mary Margaret took over for two weeks, via remote broadcasts. From the subsequent fan mail and ratings, it was clear that not only did her fans remember her but that young listeners had discovered why.

At home in the Catskills. *Anselma Dell'Olio*

One of Columbia Broadcasting's hottest properties, 1938. *CBS Radio*

JIMMY FIDLER

Hollywood's first gossip columnist was born in 1900 in Memphis, Tennessee. Jimmy became interested in movies while he was in the Marine Corps during World War I. Mustered out in 1919, he headed for Hollywood where he planned to become a star. Under the name James Marion (his middle name) he appeared in a few features, one a Wallace Reid starrer in which Jimmy played Reid's brother. By 1920 he felt he would never make it as an actor. He went into publicity and became Sid Grauman's publicity manager for his Million Dollar Theatre in downtown Los Angeles. He did so well that he was offered a job at $22.50 a week as managing editor of the *Hollywood News*.

It was the early twenties when the infamous scandals about silent stars were breaking in newspapers around the world. Fidler, who has always fancied himself as somewhat of a crusader, began a front page "clean up Hollywood" campaign, including a good many sordid stories of Paramount contract players (such as Mary Miles Minter, who has lived in Santa Monica, California, in total seclusion ever since). When the studio offered him $75 a week to promote Gloria Swanson, Fidler jumped at the chance. Before his first day was out, he learned that the front office had only wanted him off the *News*—and the average tenure in his new job was about three weeks! Jimmy went straight to Swanson and told her the full story. She liked his honesty and worked with him, beginning a close friendship that has lasted to this day.

When Swanson went independent, Jimmy opened his own publicity firm and did very well, until the stock market crash of 1929 wiped him out along with everyone else. Deciding not to renew his public relations career because he never liked it anyway, he landed a spot on a radio show called "Hollywood on the Air." He did his first broadcast in 1932, a short interview with

Dorothy Jordan (now living in Pacific Palisades, California, married to producer Merian C. Cooper). "We were both terrible!" says Fidler. Jimmy's real forte proved to be gossip. Not only was he a genius at collecting it but he had a very distinctive voice, with a delivery not unlike Walter Winchell's. It all started one day when the program ran a minute under, and the network was stuck with sixty seconds of silence. Fidler proposed that any recurrent void be filled with one-sentence blurbs about the stars. It wasn't long before he had his own show "dishing the dirt" about the stars and their films, to which he would award merits in the form of bells. "It's a four-bell picture," Jimmy would announce, ringing a bell close to the microphone. His original sponsor was Tangee lipstick, but he is probably best remembered for popularizing Arrid deodorant.

Fidler managed to keep on good terms with his archrivals Hedda Hopper and Louella Parson (who has been in a sanitarium for a number of years), except for the time he scooped them on the Jon Hall–Frances Langford elopement. He upset others though. Constance Bennett threatened to sue him after one of his "open letters" to her. W. C. Fields was incensed after Jimmy told the world how Fields, supposedly undergoing a rest cure for alcoholism, was having liquor smuggled in to him by the very men the studio was paying to watch him. Jimmy had his troubles with the film makers also. All the major studios at one time or another barred him. He claims never to have been bothered by this because the studio employees would provide him with more news than ever just to ingratiate themselves, to indulge themselves in what Fidler calls the gossip urge. Many, he maintains, just want to tell something and then see it in print.

Jimmy's network radio program went off the air in the early fifties. However, he has never stopped broadcasting. From an office in North Hollywood, the only man to interview Greta Garbo on the air ("A very duddy sort of affair," Jimmy called it recently) records news flashes about Hollywood stars that he sells to radio stations around the country, though mostly in smaller towns, especially in the South. He has had serious trouble with his eyesight but continues to work six and sometimes seven days a week.

In his North Hollywood office.
Clifford May

With Paramount Pictures, 1930.

LILLIAN ROTH

The world-famous alcoholic was born in 1910 in New York City. Her real name is Lillian (after Lillian Russell) Rutstein. In 1916 Lillian's mother took her to Educational Pictures, where she became their trademark—a living "statue" holding the lamp of knowledge. The next year, she made her Broadway debut in *The Inner Man*. She debuted in motion pictures in *Pershing's Crusaders* (1918). At Professional Children's School her classmates were Ruby Keeler,* Penny Singleton,** Patsy Kelly,* and Milton Berle. At ten, Lillian, nicknamed "Butterfingers" by friends, appeared on Broadway with a fifty-page part in *Shavings*. She was billed as "Broadway's Youngest Star." Thereafter, Lillian and her sister Ann toured the Keith Circuit as Lillian Roth and Co.; another of their billings was "The Roth Kids." A high point for the girls was when they were taken to meet President Woodrow Wilson.

When Lillian entered the Clark School of Concentration in the early twenties she had a one-thousand-dollar wardrobe. She appeared in *Artists and Models* in 1923 (she told the management that she was nineteen years old). After that she went into *Revels* with the late Frank Fay. At seventeen Lillian did the first of three *Earl Carroll Vanities* with Ray Dooley. She was also featured in Flo Ziegfeld's *Midnight Frolics* right after that.

In the meantime Lillian signed a seven-year contract with Paramount and appeared in such films as *The Love Parade* (1929) with Maurice Chevalier, *Honey* (1930) in which she introduced "Sing You Sinners," *Paramount on Parade* (1930), *Madam Satan* (1930) with the late Reginald Denny, and *Animal Crackers* (1930) with the Marx Brothers. (Zeppo Marx is retired and lives in Los Angeles.)

Lillian left Paramount in 1930 to free-lance. When she arrived in New York to play the Palace she found three of her movies playing on Broadway. She was a big name in movies and on the stage, and appeared in *Earl Carroll Vanities* in 1931 and 1932. Lillian was an accomplished singer in a period when nearly everything was being set to music.

Unfortunately, her personal life and alcohol got in the way of everything she did. She says her parents were not a stage mother and father but

24

because of them she developed a life pattern of relying on other people, usually husbands, to handle her money, contracts, etc.

Lillian seemed to vanish during the late thirties until 1953 when she appeared on television on Ralph Edwards's *This Is Your Life*. After the nation heard her story of alcoholism, over forty thousand letters poured in, and her autobiography *I'll Cry Tomorrow* was published the following year. The book became a worldwide best seller that sold over 7 million copies in twenty languages. In 1954 a movie version was made, featuring Susan Hayward as Lillian. It was a huge success, and once again Lillian began to play nightclubs and made television appearances singing the songs she originally made famous: "When the Red, Red, Robin Comes Bob, Bob, Bobbin' Along," "I'd Climb the Highest Mountain," and others. She was earning twelve thousand dollars a week and getting as many as ten thousand letters a week from her readers. In 1958 her second book, *Beyond My Worth*, was published but it did not do as well.

Lillian's earlier marriages were to aviator William C. Scott, Willie Richards, an air force cadet, Judge Benjamin Shalleck, Eugene J. Weiner, and Edward Goldman, all divorced. Then in 1955 she met Thomas Burt McGuire, scion of Funk and Wagnalls Publishing Co., at a meeting of Alcoholics Anonymous, of which she was a member since 1946. He married her and became her manager, until September 1963 when she received a note from him from Phoenix telling her it was all over. According to Lillian, he was living with another woman who bore him a child, and he had taken every cent from their joint bank-account and left her broke.

Lillian resumed her drinking. Though her 301-performance Broadway run in *I Can Get It for You Wholesale* in 1962 had given her great encouragement, the only work she has had since her breakup was in the road company of *Funny Girl*, in 1964. She claims that *Funny Girl*'s cast unjustly accused her of drinking, which hurt her very much, and that it damaged her reputation. She swears that she has stopped drinking for good.

Lillian shares a penthouse on Manhattan's West Fifty-eighth Street with a woman, three poodles, a police dog, a Chihuahua, and three dachshunds. She hopes to work again as an actress or singer but has been restricted lately to such jobs as bakery employee, hospital attendant, and package wrapper.

Still smiling, WBAI–FM, New York City. *John G. Gilligan*

Arthur and a partner demon-
strating the Charleston, popular
in the twenties. *UPI*

ARTHUR MURRAY

America's Dancing Master was born Arthur Murray Teichman on New York's Lower East Side in 1895. His first recollection of dancing was when a girl noticed his shyness at a school dance and coaxed him into trying a few steps with her. In no time Arthur felt he could dance pretty well and crashed all the immigrant weddings in his neighborhood, thus learning all the steps of the various nationalities. He then enrolled at Castle House, a chain of dancing schools owned by Irene Castle.* He proved such an adept pupil that shortly he became an instructor.

Upon completion of high school, Arthur took a four-year course in business administration at Georgia Institute of Technology. But upon graduation he returned to dancing—the Baroness de Cuddelston took him with her to Asheville, North Carolina, where she ran dancing academies at the hotels. Arthur was paid one hundred dollars weekly, but he had an idea of his own and after a short while left for New York City.

In 1923 he took a one-room office at 229 Broadway and ran ads headlined How I Became Popular Overnight. In them he promised to make anyone who subscribed to his mail-order school an expert fox-trot dancer in no time. Some forty thousand people replied.

Murray, who has been described as looking like a retired undertaker, opened a school that soon mushroomed into several schools in several cities. He hired instructors and concentrated on the business end, including promotion. He proved a genius at both. By 1941 his yearly gross was $2 million. By 1951 it had risen to $22 million. When he sold out his interests in 1964 to several men who had owned Arthur Murray franchises, the annual gross from schools as far away as South Africa, Australia, and Germany, as well as in every major city in North America, was $55 million.

The biggest boom for his schools was the advent of television. His *Arthur Murray Party* began in 1950 as a summer replacement. It took until 1958 to get a sponsor for it, but by that time it was trouncing its competition, *Desilu Playhouse,* 24.7 to 18.7 in the ratings. Since Arthur's personality is somewhat flat and he speaks with a lisp, most of the on-camera chores fell to his wife, the former Kathryn Kohnfelder, whom he married in 1925. In spite of her voice, which someone said sounded like that of a long-distance operator, she was quite popular.

Even before people at home could see couples dancing, the Murrays promoted their schools on radio. During the forties, the hit song "Arthur Murray Taught Me Dancing in a Hurray" made his method and name household words. Two presidential candidates took lessons at the Murray studios. Both learned to dance but neither was elected. Eleanor Roosevelt took rumba lessons at the Washington, D.C., studios. Murray claims that the only people he has not been able to teach were mental defectives. He seldom took a private pupil. One exception was heiress Eleanor Close Hutton, who paid him five thousand dollars for the course.

He has written three books: *How to Become a Good Dancer,* with K. K. Murray, *Arthur Murray's Dance Secrets,* and *Let's Dance.* The Murrays have a large and very valuable collection of modern paintings.

Until they retired from their 452 schools the Murrays, who have twins, Phyllis and Jane, were very much a part of the Manhattan social scene. From their home in Honolulu they still visit New York for large charity balls or an occasional television appearance. On Anne Bancroft's CBS special in 1970, Murray danced briefly with the star. Asked recently if their life had changed much since moving to the islands, Kathryn replied: "A little. Arthur doesn't have to wear a tux very often but we still do a lot of dancing."

On a recent television show. *CBS Television*

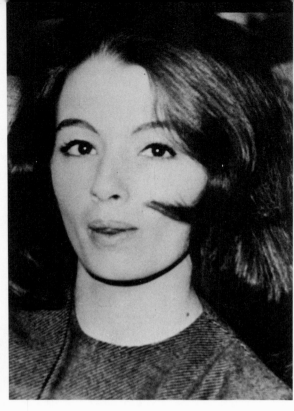

The famous leaving-for-court photo that appeared on newspaper front pages all over the world in 1963. *UPI*

CHRISTINE KEELER

The girl whose sex life brought down England's Tory government in 1963 was born in 1942. For most of her early years she lived with her mother and stepfather, Ted Huish, in a converted railway carriage and earned her own money baby-sitting. She quickly discovered how attractive she was to men: the fathers of her charges made passes when she was alone in the house. In her midteens "a black sweeper" seduced her and a GI impregnated her. Because she found the ways of the world hard for an uneducated working-class girl, she gravitated toward a career in prostitution.

After free-lancing for a while, she was introduced by a wealthy Arab to osteopath Stephen Ward. Ward was socially prominent in London and regularly introduced girls like Christine to rich, usually older, men. It was all very discreet and the fees were impressive, but what it boiled down to was that Ward pimped for several stunning girls.

The entire affair became public through a very indirect incident. One of Christine's castoffs in a fit of jealousy fired several shots into the door of her West End flat. He was arrested, and she was summoned as a witness in his trial. When she did not appear, British newspapers, knowing her complete background but unable to print anything outright because of England's strict libel laws, hinted that Christine declined to testify because of her sordid personal life involving a number of celebrities. One was John Profumo, one of the most respected members of the English establishment.

On the floor of the House of Commons he denied that there had been "impropriety between myself and Miss Keeler." Investigation proved different, and he was forced to resign his position of war minister. Particularly damaging to his case was the revelation that during the time she had been seeing Profumo, Christine had also slept with the handsome Soviet spy Eugene "Honey Bear" Ivanov. Ivanov was returned to Russia and has not been heard from since. But Profumo went on to build a solid reputation during the past few years working with poverty-stricken Londoners in the East End. He is still married to British actress Valerie Hobson, whose career following the scandal has come to a standstill. Dr. Ward was not overlooked. He was brought to trial but just hours before the jury brought in its verdict he committed suicide.

The Conservative party lost its majority in the next general election and few would deny that the scandal figured prominently in the voters' decision. For her part in the affair, Christine served nine months in prison for perjury: she had testified that her old boyfriend had beaten her. Diplomats, cabinet ministers, and other luminaries breathed easier when all parties stopped talking publicly.

Some of the most damaging testimony was provided by Mandy Rice-Davies who emerged nearly as famous as Christine. Until their stories were revealed, the girls had been close friends and roommates.

Christine thereafter married a good-looking engineer named James Levermore. Recently, James filed for divorce, charging desertion. Miss Keeler and their four-year-old son, Jimmy, live in a London apartment. The English tabloid *News of the World* not long ago paid her twenty thousand pounds for the serialization rights to her autobiography, and book rights were offered to publishers; those who could afford it were leery of being associated with such a tasteless project.

At a recent London party (left to right) : Christine, photographer David Bailey, actress Penelope Tree, singer Marianne Faithfull. *UPI*

At twenty, plugging her autobiography, 1964. *UPI*

MANDY RICE-DAVIES

Christine Keeler's partner in vice was born in Birmingham, England, in 1944. She left school at fifteen and spent a year as a local shopgirl before moving to London; the one-way ticket to the capital was Mandy's sixteenth birthday present to herself. She worked for a short time as a waitress before meeting Christine Keeler. The two hit it off and soon took a flat together, and in six months the pretty blond was the mistress of a wealthy Englishman who gave her a number of gifts, including a mink coat and a Jaguar.

As he had been doing for Miss Keeler, Dr. Stephen Ward, the elegant procurer, arranged meetings for Miss Rice-Davies with the rich and powerful. Among her seventeenth-birthday gifts were some dazzling diamonds; and the fashionable artist Joseph Diftler was commissioned to paint her portrait. Mandy's dates, like her roommate's, though not always famous and powerful, were nevertheless always very rich.

When the international scandal broke two years later, Mandy was called to testify about her activities. On and off the witness stand she proved to be excellent copy for the tabloids. She seemed not a bit embarrassed by the publicity and to actually enjoy the interviews with newspapermen.

At one point on the stand, Mandy held the courtroom spellbound as she related how at a London orgy she was paid one pound per stroke for whipping her host, who appeared stark naked except for a mask. Flagellation, she said, was very common among the clients she entertained at Dr. Ward's. Another startling revelation was that the bedrooms in which the girls received their "johns" were usually equipped with two-way mirrors.

Because she was under the constant surveillance of the police once her profession was known, Mandy moved to Munich, where she headlined in a nightclub. "Because my name is Mandy Rice-Davies," she said, "I have to start at the top." Her opening number was "Diamonds Are a Girl's Best Friend" followed by "An Englishman Needs Time."

Her side of the sordid story was published in magazine format as *The Mandy Report*. Though it was only a year following the party girl's appearance on the world's front pages, the *Report*'s reception was less than enthusiastic. At a party she gave for one hundred and fifty "friends," only her publishers—and some press—turned up.

In 1966 Mandy became the wife of twenty-six-year-old Rafael Shaul, then working as an Israeli airline steward. Shortly afterward he became a pilot. The couple had met several months earlier when Mandy was appearing in a Tel Aviv cabaret. The following year Shaul's family, who already owned several cafes in Israel, opened one in Tel Aviv called "Mandy's."

In 1968 the Shauls became parents of a baby girl. Mandy, who has converted to Judaism, visits London occasionally on modeling jobs. She says she has not seen Profumo or Christine in a long time and claims to be very happy in Tel Aviv. Of her husband, she says: "He knows everything," but then so does everyone else.

Modeling a "Yo-Yo" bikini recently. *UPI*

A 1951 portrait publicizing *The Story of Will Rogers.*

WILL ROGERS, JR.

The oldest child of the internationally famous humorist was born in New York City in 1911. His father was performing his popular rope tricks and commenting on the happenings of the day in vaudeville and considering offers by Flo Ziegfeld to star in his *Follies.*

When Will, Jr., was eight years old the Rogers family moved to Beverly Hills, California, where he attended school. At Stanford he majored in journalism, edited the school paper, and won awards for his polo playing, swimming, and debating. In 1935 he graduated. Also that year his father was killed in an airplane crash with Wiley Post.

Upon graduation, Will with his brother and sister purchased control of the *Beverly-Hills Citizen.* Will took over as publisher and editor-in-chief. In a short time, the Rogerses had made the newspaper a lively and successful daily, with objective reporting and enlightened editorials, mostly written by Will.

In 1942 he filed for Congress from the sixteenth district in the Democratic primary, and was almost immediately inducted into the army. But although he did not make one campaign speech, his family and friends worked so diligently that he was elected. He was released from service and spent a year in the House of Representatives, voting for anti-poll-tax legislation and for the establishment of the United Nations. As a young liberal in an anti-FDR Congress, Rogers made quite a name for himself in a very short time. His first speech on the floor was an eloquent attack against a powerful congressman, Martin Dies.*

Rogers resigned his seat in 1944 and served as a second lieutenant with a tank destroyer in Italy, France, and Belgium, for which he received the Bronze Star for heroism and a promotion to first lieutenant. After being wounded in the Battle of the Bulge he received the Purple Heart.

In 1946 he ran against William F. Knowland * for the Senate seat from California but was defeated.

For many years Rogers has been honorary chairman of ARROW (American Restitution and Rights of Old Wrongs), an organization actively promoting Indian causes. For a short time in the late fifties he was chairman of the California State Parks Commission.

In the 1952 film *The Story of Will Rogers* he played his father with much of the warmth and charm that had made the senior Rogers perhaps the best-liked man in the world. Critics and audiences marveled at the similarity of their mannerisms, speech, and stance. There was no acting involved. Like his father, he is a man totally unpretentious and deeply concerned about the world. His smile and sense of humor remind even his father's old friends of the senior Rogers.

In 1953 he did a radio series for CBS entitled *Rogers of the Gazette,* and in 1956 did an early morning television show called *Good Morning!* He was seen in two other films, *The Boy from Oklahoma* (1954), and *Wild Heritage* (1958), but had no interest in pursuing a screen career.

In 1968 Rogers was made special assistant to the commissioner of the Bureau of Indian Affairs. He maintained an office in Washington but spent much of his time traveling about Indian reservations and reporting on conditions. He resigned the position in June 1969 but is often called on by the present Indian commissioner, who is a close friend.

Rogers lives in Beverly Hills, where he also maintains an office, but keeps another house in Malibu and a large ranch in Oklahoma that belonged to his father. He and his wife, the former Collier Connell, were married in 1940 and have two adopted children, Clem, twenty-five, and Carl, nineteen, both Indians. Rogers inherited some Navajo blood from his father, who had always stated his pride in his Indian heritage.

Methodist Rogers has skillfully managed the considerable real estate holdings left to his family by his father, and is active in Democratic party politics behind the scenes. Despite his varied interests and activities, when asked recently by an interviewer what he was doing, Rogers answered with typical family understatement: "Not a damn thing worth mentioning."

Beside an old Indian map in his Beverly Hills office. *Clifford May*

In 1952, one of the hottest singers around.

DOROTHY COLLINS

The star of television's *Your Hit Parade* was born in Windsor, Ontario, in 1926. Her father worked for Chrysler Motors across the river in Detroit. Dorothy, whose real name is Marjorie Chandler, disliked her given name and took her sister's. Her mother had experienced some opera training and expected Dorothy's sister to sing, while discouraging Dorothy because she considered Dorothy's voice quite irritating. Dorothy believed her mother and planned to become a secretary but then, at age twelve, she won an amateur contest, with a wristwatch as first prize. Thereafter she started singing regularly on *Uncle Nick's Children's Hour* on WJBK. In 1942 she auditioned for Raymond Scott, the orchestra leader, who persuaded her mother to bring the girl to Chicago where she could live with him and his family and study singing. Five years later she was singing in the Raymond Scott Quintet.

On the death of Mark Warnow, the music director for *Your Hit Parade,* Lucky Strike hired his brother, Harry Warnow, known as Raymond Scott, to take over what was then a radio program. In 1949, Scott signed Dorothy to sing the show's commercial "Be Happy, Go Lucky." When the show went on television in 1950, Dorothy was one of the featured vocalists and continued to do the commercials inside the Lucky Strike bullseye.

Dorothy's image on the show derived in part from an old blouse. The agency wanted to have one made especially for her but time was pressing and so she wore the one that had seen countless one-night stands. It was a simple white pleated-front affair, inexpensive and easy to launder, and she wore it with a narrow black velvet ribbon crossed at the neck. That blouse became nearly as famous as Dorothy, and was marketed throughout the country. It was exactly in keeping with the image the cigarette company wanted for her, sweet and simple.

For seven years Dorothy was the show's female star, singing with Russell Arms (who lives with his wife and family on Sunset Plaza Drive in Los Angeles) and Snooky Lanson (who does a daily television show in Shreveport, Louisiana). For several years the show was similarly cast on television and radio, except for the 1957 season. The program tried a change of cast, dropping Dorothy, but the public rejected it and the originals were restored in 1958, continuing through the final telecast April 24, 1959. "It was really like a big family," said Dorothy recently. "I know that sounds corny but everyone connected with the show liked each other. I think it came over that way." In the meantime, Dorothy had married the divorced Raymond Scott in 1952.

After *Your Hit Parade* Dorothy worked for big money in clubs throughout the country. Her appearances in Las Vegas, but as a sexy chanteuse now, were so successful that the management gave her a diamond watch on one occasion and a solid gold bracelet on another. She auditioned for the musical *She Loves Me* in 1963 but lost out. "It was the only thing in my professional life that I ever really wanted," she said. In 1960 Dorothy was a regular on television's *Candid Camera*.

Dorothy still is a draw at strawhat theatre around the country. In recent years, she has starred in *The Unsinkable Molly Brown, South Pacific, Most Happy Fella,* and *Do I Hear a Waltz?*

In 1965 Dorothy and Raymond were divorced. She had two children by him. The fifty-six-year-old musician agreed to pay fifty dollars per month in child support. The following year Dorothy married actor Ron Holgate, whom she had met in summer stock. This marriage was indeed a contrast. Having lived thirteen years with a man many years her senior she now was the wife of a man eleven years her junior. "I had never dated, flirted, or been courted in my life when I met Ron," she told an interviewer. "Emotionally I was seventeen. It is awfully nice to find out what it is to be a woman."

The Holgates live in the small town of Montvale, New Jersey, only thirty-five minutes by car from New York. Her husband was nominated in 1969 for an award for his performance in the hit musical *1776*. Dorothy, who does all her own housework and loves it, had a baby girl, their first, in 1968. To this day, the girl who has probably sold more cigarettes than anyone, with the exception of Philip Morris's Johnny,* has never smoked one.

As she looks today. *Diana Keyt*

Middleweight Champion of the World, 1941.

TONY ZALE

Boxing's Man of Steel was born to Polish parents in Gary, Indiana, in 1914. Young Tony received very little education and then went to work in the local steel mills—until the early thirties when he began fighting professionally.

He made a slow, steady rise among the ranks of the middleweights but there was nothing spectacular about him either in style or in record. In 1934 he had sixteen wins against five losses, and during the next two years, though he returned to the mills, was lured into the ring fourteen times, winning eleven. After that, he began to acquire a reputation for knocking out opponents: in 1939, in eight bouts, he KO'd six, took a seventh, and lost one. In 1940 he had only one loss and four of his six wins were knockouts. In 1941 he won all of his seven matches, five of them knockouts.

In 1941 the middleweight crown had been in dispute for eleven years, with the New York Boxing Association, in opposition to the National Boxing Association, supporting Billy Soose as the champion. But that year Soose gave up his crown to enter the lightweight division and Georgie Abrams, who had beaten Soose on three occasions, was matched against Tony Zale for the title. They fought on November 28, 1941, and when Tony walked out of the ring he was World Middleweight Champ. He remained the champ for six years, with his most dramatic title defense occurring on July 26, 1946, when he KO'd Rocky Graziano for a winner's purse of $78,892.87. But the next time they met, July 16, 1947, Graziano reciprocated in the sixth round. Up to then, as champ, Tony had walked away with $140,682.46. Less than a year later, June 10, 1948, the two faced each other again and Tony KO'd Graziano to regain his title, taking only $60,000 as the challenger's share. His title was wrested from him September 21, 1948, by the late French pugilist Marcel Cerdan when Zale was unable to leave his corner at the beginning of the twelfth round. Tony hung up his gloves after that, commenting later that he could have won but "my right elbow was hurtin'." The doctor who operated on the elbow after the fight said that if Tony had delayed much longer he would have lost the arm.

These days Tony, whose money and famous friends are gone, is a caricature of his old self. His eyes, once an attractive blue, are milky gray and peer out from slits, and his speech, according to one reporter, is "not quite marbles in his mouth, but it isn't always easy to understand him." The veteran of three hundred fights spends a few nights every week sparring with youngsters at the Mission of Our Lady of Mercy, a parish clubhouse in a tough Chicago neighborhood. For a while he held a job as greeter at Gallagher's Steak House in New York City but returned to Chicago to train youngsters to box. "This is where I belong," he said. "It's all I know." He does not understand why boys today do not care to get roughed up in his profession and describes his protégés as "not hungry enough. They really don't want to fight much." He expresses contempt for such champions of today as Muhummed Ali and Sonny Liston.

Tony lives on the fourth floor of a walk-up YMCA and holds the title of head boxing coach of the Catholic Youth Organization. He has a wife from whom he has been separated for some time and two daughters, whom he hasn't seen in years.

The pride of his life are his weight (he keeps it at 168 pounds, only 8 pounds over the middleweight limit) and his memories ("They can't take that away," he says) .

Keeping down the weight today by daily workouts. *UPI*

In the film *The Fabulous Dorseys,* 1947 (left to right) : Connie Haines, Tommy Dorsey, Helen O'Connell, and Jimmy Dorsey.

HELEN O'CONNELL

The pert, dimpled songstress of the 1940s was born in Lima, Ohio, in 1921 to nonprofessional parents. She made up her mind at age thirteen to sing with a band and landed a job a few years later with Jimmy Richard. Helen was still in her teens when Bill Burton, Jimmy Dorsey's personal manager, discovered her singing with Larry Funk and His Band of a Thousand Melodies at the Village Barn in Greenwich Village. Dorsey signed her to replace Ella Mae Morse in 1939 when, after only a month, the black singer proved unable to work harmoniously with his organization.

Helen was hailed immediately by musicians and fans alike. The band enjoyed her pleasant disposition, and everyone was taken by her obvious assets—blond hair and one of the warmest smiles in show business. If Helen was less sultry than some of her contemporaries such as Helen Forrest (living in Los Angeles) or Martha Tilton (retired and living with her family in the Mandeville Canyon area of Los Angeles), it was not because she lacked sex appeal. True, her girl-next-door image was less competition than Peggy Lee might have provided but "nice girls" were in vogue during the war years and Helen epitomized the pretty, sweet young thing millions of young men wanted to settle down with. That she could sing well didn't hurt either, even though George Simon, author of *The Big Bands,* who liked her personally, felt that she "had a tendency to overprhase and not always to sing in tune." However, Simon records, the public adored her. She won *Metronome*'s poll for top female vocalist of 1940, holding the honor among trade papers for two more years.

After two years of solos with Dorsey in such top spots as the Terrace

Room of the Hotel New Yorker, Helen began singing with Bob Eberle (living in Great Neck, Long Island, New York). Their duets became the popular aspect of a radio program on which Dorsey appeared weekly. The show was sponsored by 20 Grand Cigarettes (they sold at ten cents a pack). Helen and Eberle dated a lot until the early forties, when he married Florine Callahan and Helen began seeing a lot of Jimmy Blumenstock, a Fordham football star.

Some of the songs she popularized were the biggest hits of the day: "Amapola," "Six Lessons from Madame La Zonga," "Embraceable You," and "Little Curly Hair in a High Chair." Probably she is most closely associated with "Green Eyes." Helen, whose eyes are hazel, recorded it when a twenty-five-thousand-record sale was considered a hit. "Green Eyes" sold ninety thousand copies in the first few days of its release.

Helen retired in 1943 after her first marriage, a marriage categorized by a contemporary as disastrous. Her second husband was Tom Chamales, who wrote *Never So Few*. On two occasions there were newspaper reports that the novelist had been jailed on wife-beating charges. From 1957 when they were married until the writer burned to death in March 1960, police were called to their home on at least five occasions. Helen met her third husband, Bob Paris, when he began dating her twenty-year-old daughter, Jackie. After their ten-month marriage was annulled in October 1965, Paris, according to local papers, resumed his dates with Jackie.

During the early fifties for a couple of years, Helen was hostess on NBC's *Today Show*, but never sang a note, and in the summer of 1956 sang with Russ Morgan's orchestra for three months on a network television show. During the past few years she has again become active in club work and commercials. In 1968 she appeared for Polaroid at Marineland in television spots seen around the nation and recently toured with Vic Damone. Following that, Helen was pitchwoman for a boxed set of reissued records of the hits of the 1940s advertised nationwide on late-night television.

When not playing places like Manhattan's Rainbow Grill or Chicago's Drake Hotel, Helen lives on Dorothy Street in Brentwood, California. She has four grown daughters and two grandchildren.

At a recent nightclub appearance.

In 1941, as usual, among the top ten in the rating polls. *NBC Radio*

FIBBER McGEE: Jim Jordan

The surviving half of the famous radio couple was born in Peoria, Illinois, in 1897. He and "Molly" Marian Driscoll first worked together singing in the local church choir. They were married in 1918, just before he entered the army.

Later they performed together in vaudeville and in 1926 broke into radio with a show called *The O'Henry Twins,* which netted them ten dollars a week from the Chicago station carrying it. It was no great success and they returned to vaudeville. In 1931 they tried again with *The Smackouts.* Jim played a small-town grocer with a penchant for telling stories and he always seemed "smack out" of anything the customer wanted.

The idea for *Fibber McGee and Molly* was developed after they met and collaborated with a writer named Don Quinn. The program was sponsored by Johnson's Wax Company and went on the air in 1935. It was a great hit from the beginning. For over twenty-two years every Tuesday night America listened to the fictional couple at home at 79 Wistful Vista. One gag became their trademark when Fibber would open a stuffed closet, it was a sound effects man's dream as the contents poured out, ending with the gentle tinkle of a bell, and deafening applause. Fibber McGee and Molly's expressions became part of the American language. Fibber's strongest curse was, "Dat rat that dat ratted!" and when one of his jokes bombed Molly would chide him with, " 'Tain't funny, McGee." Her favorite lament was "heavenly days," which was also the title of one of their movies, made in 1944. Their other films were *This Way Please* (1937), *Look Who's Laughing* (1941), and *Here We Go Again* (1942).

Their supporting characters were just as funny. Fictional neighbor Throckmorton P. Gildersleeve began to rival them in popularity until he (Hal Peary, now managing his real estate holdings in Manhattan Beach, California) played the character on a series of his own on the same network, and it was the same with the maid, Beulah, who was originally played by Marlin Hurt. Others on the show were Mayor La Trivia, The Old Timer (originated by Cliff Arquette), Wallace Wimple, who brought shrieks from the audience with his constant references to his big old wife, and Sis, the little girl next door (played by Molly), with her repeated "Whatcha doin', mister?"

In 1953 Molly suffered a heart attack, which ruled out the couple's appearing on the television series, which existed only for the 1959 season and starred Cathy Lewis and Bob Sweeney. The radio series went off the air in 1957. Fibber and Molly then did short bits of their comedy for *Monitor*, the NBC weekend radio program, for a couple of years. Fibber's last appearance was with Jack Paar in 1961, the year Molly died of cancer. In 1962 the widower married his present wife, Gretchen, the widow of dialect comedian Harry Stewart. The large estate Fibber and Molly had always maintained in Encino was sold, and the newlyweds moved into a smaller home on Hazen Drive in West Los Angeles where they live today. Jim Jordan has multiplied his *Fibber* earnings many times over through shrewd manipulations in real estate and has found time for himself and his wife to visit Europe and Africa in the last few years. His son, a successful television director, and daughter by his first marriage have presented him with grandchildren. One of Jim, Jr.'s, credits was the syndicated *Donald O'Connor Show*. Although Jim is proud that his work with his late wife is so well remembered, he has no desire to dwell on it. He considers himself completely retired and no longer grants interviews. One of his closest friends is Charles Correll * (Andy on the *Amos 'n' Andy* radio series).

At the Radio Pioneers of America testimonial dinner in his honor. *Jon Virzi*

In 1950, still a familiar voice on radio. *NBC Radio*

CLIFTON FADIMAN

The author, editor, and critic and the moderator of radio's *Information Please* was born in Brooklyn in 1904. His Russian immigrant father was a druggist, his mother, a nurse. Older brother Edwin, who now manages his business affairs, taught Clifton geography by his fifth birthday. By the time Clifton, or Kip, was ten, he had read Homer, Dante, Sophocles, and Milton. (His family nicknamed him Kip after an extended attack of hiccups.) For a while he worked as a soda jerk in his father's drugstore, as a ship chandler, and as an officer for the French-American Line. While at Columbia University, Clifton and Edwin, delivery boy and editor-publisher respectively, ran the *Forest Hills Reporter* and managed a bookshop in Pennsylvania Station. Before graduating Phi Beta Kappa in 1925, Kip had averaged a minimum of one thousand dollars annually, part of which came from writing book reviews for *The Nation*.

For two years Fadiman taught English at the Ethical Culture High School. After that he joined Simon & Schuster as an assistant editor, was promoted in 1929 to full editor, eventually became editor-in-chief, resigned, and continued as an outside editorial adviser. In 1929, one of the books Clifton had suggested for publication, *Trader Horn*, became a national best seller and it was bought by Metro-Goldwyn-Mayer. For a decade beginning in 1933 he was book editor of *The New Yorker* magazine.

His career as a radio personality began in 1934 reviewing books over the air. The program flopped. Four years later he began *Information Please,* which soon had an audience of 9 million every Friday evening and was praised by the critics for bringing intellectualism to the masses. The program opened with a crowing rooster followed by a challenge from the announcer: "Wake up, America! It's time to stump the experts!" The original panel included Franklin P. Adams and John Kieran. Oscar Levant was added later, when Fadiman became the moderator. A question from the radio audience that stumped the experts merited a set of the *Encyclopaedia*

Britannica. The program lasted fourteen years. In between writing and anthologizing books on literature, Fadiman was also emcee and quizmaster of radio's *Quiz Kids, This Is Show Business, Mathematics,* and *Alumni Fun.* His personal favorite was *Conversation,* broadcast from 1954 to 1957.

Fadiman no longer teaches, lectures, or broadcasts but does contribute occasional articles and reviews to such magazines as *Holiday* and *This Week* in addition to a continuing flow of introductions to anthologies and text-books. He has done very well financially as a judge for the Book-of-the-Month Club and by lending his prestige to the Famous Writers School mail-order course for would-be writers. His publishers and some of his con-temporaries, though, were disappointed. They had great expectations that Clifton would develop into an important writer.

Clifton resides with his second wife, Annalee Whitmore Jacoby, coauthor of *Thunder Out of China* (1946), in a Bel Air mansion that once belonged to silent-film-star Coleen Moore. His study/office, which faces the large swimming pool, had formerly been used as a projection room. His first mar-riage was to Pauline Elizabeth Rush, from 1927 to 1949 when they were divorced.

Few minds have been so admired by middle-America as Clifton Fadiman's. His accomplishments today, however, seem far less impressive than thirty years ago when a college education was still the exception. He had a sharp eye for what the buying public would pay to read and an enormous fund of facts stored in an exceptional memory. But there is little in his career to prove that his knowledge was coupled with imagination or creativity.

Fadiman is fascinated by the art of conversation and feels it is practiced less and less lately. He rates Fredric March as one of the few theatrical per-sonalities who is a good conversationalist. Clifton, who has throughout his career displayed a knack for keeping abreast of trends among intellectuals, seemed more than a little behind the times recently when he told an in-terviewer that women were almost never good talkers.

Fadiman has often been quoted as saying, "I am not a profound thinker." No arguments have been heard.

Snapped recently in his Bel Air home.
Clifford May

Observing the Kremlin during a 1954 trip to the Soviet Union. *UPI*

MIKE ROMANOFF

The bogus prince and restaurateur's background is so full of fantastic exaggerations, deceptions, and half-truths that no one knows the real story. According to reliable sources, he has used the names William A. Wellington, Count Gladstone, Arthur Wellesley, and Arthur Edward Willoughby. Some say he was born in Vilna, Russia, in 1890. Mike says he was born in the United States but returned to Russia while still a child. There is some evidence that he was brought up in a series of orphan asylums in Texas, Illinois, and New York. He claims to have served as a cossack colonel on the eastern front during World War I. At other times he was supposedly an officer with Allenby in Palestine, an ambulance driver for the French, and imprisoned for killing a German nobleman in a duel.

Theories abound about his real name and origin but most seem to agree that he was born Harry F. Gerguson, probably in Brooklyn, in 1895. The earliest supportable facts available on him date to when he turned up in Paris in 1919 with adequate clothes, luggage, and a knowledge of French to pass himself off as His Imperial Highness, the Prince Michael Alexandrovitch Dmitri Obolensky Romanoff, nephew of the last of the czars of all the Russias. From there he traveled to London where all went well until he was jailed for refusal to pay his bills. Mike arrived on Ellis Island in 1922 but was detained when he could not prove his place of birth. He escaped and arrived in Manhattan amidst a blaze of publicity. Even the *New York Times* treated him seriously.

He embarked on a successful lecture tour, spinning tales about his days in the French Foreign Legion, of his witnessing Rasputin's assassination, or the Bolsheviks who he claimed still threatened his life. There were some minor difficulties with the authorities in the next few years. Important people found small expensive things missing after his visits, checks bounced, and the prince along with entourage attended functions to which he had never been invited. In the false and superficial world it is not rewarding to be exposed as either.

Eventually and inevitably, in 1927, Mike Romanoff appeared in Hollywood. The movie community welcomed the spectacular fake with open arms. He was invited to parties to give them tone and was paid handsomely as a technical adviser on pictures with foreign locales being shot on the back lots of studios.

The success of his restaurant—opened in 1938 and financed anonymously by several big names in Hollywood—gave him money, more fame, and a brush with respectability. The Hollywood establishment adored being put down by the haughty little fraud, and no one, not even the real gourmets, dared question the quality of Mike's cuisine. For a time there were Romanoff restaurants in San Francisco, which failed, and in Palm Springs. Until it closed in 1962, Romanoff's was the place to been seen if you were a star. But by then the days of such overpriced and pretentious establishments were over. The prince slipped quietly into exile with his former secretary Gloria Lister, his wife since 1948.

In 1958 the United States government had given up its attempt to deport him and he was sworn in as a citizen—after renouncing for all times his claims to the title that had made him a living legend.

The Romanoffs, who have no children, live in Beverly Hills on North Beverly Drive. Mike is still close friends with Frank Sinatra and played a brief role in Frank's *Tony Rome* (1967). During its production a young actor who had been briefed on Romanoff's reputation as the most outrageous phoney in the phoney capital of the world, tried to put him on by addressing Mike in Russian. But Mike dismissed him with a look of grand disdain. Later, he said, "The vulgarity of a stranger speaking to me in that tongue! We never spoke anything but French at court."

With Frank Sinatra on the movie set of *Tony Rome*.
UPI

On a 1938 broadcast of the *Bob Hope Show.*

JERRY COLONNA

The google-eyed comedian was born Gerard Colonna in Boston, Massachusetts, in 1905. After graduating from the Boston English High School he got a job working as a longshoreman. Nights he studied music, specializing in trombone and drums. By the early thirties he had a job with the CBS staff orchestra, where he developed a reputation for making the other players break up with laughter during rehearsals, and sometimes during performances. With his wild facial contortions that always included rolling his huge popeyes Jerry could make nearly anyone who looked his way break up. Sometimes he would sing along with the band at rehearsals in a voice that has been described as "the sound of feeding time at the zoo." Not all conductors found him amusing but he was so popular among fellow musicians that they would recommend him for jobs. During warm-ups of live radio programs he often mugged for the audience.

By the midthirties Jerry was working short bits on shows with Bing Crosby, Walter O'Keefe (retired and living in Palos Verdes, California), and Fred Allen. When in 1938 Pepsodent Tooth Paste decided to present Bob Hope once a week on network radio, Colonna was added to the cast of the radio show. He became to Hope what "The Mad Russian" was to Eddie Cantor—an utterly mad character who might appear at any time, anywhere, with some ridiculous scheme or remark. In their "duologues" Hope played the straight man and Jerry got the laughs. As soon as he began walking to the microphone the studio audience would warn listeners of his approach by gales of laughter. Many preferred his zany material and absurd appearance to the glib star. His weekly salutation, "Greetings, Gate!" became a part of the American language within a short time after the program's debut. Another of his idiomatic contributions was his friend "Yehudi" who never appeared but was known all over the country. "Who's Yehudi?" Hope would ask each week, but the idiotic answer he got was usually drowned out by the laughter of the studio audience. Jerry worked in skits with Hope's guest stars as well as with the popular Vera Vague, played by Barbara Jo Allen (now Mrs. Norman Morell of Santa Barbara, California), another of Hope's regulars. Colonna was enormously popular among the GIs when Hope took his cast to army camps and naval bases throughout the world in World War II. In 1946 he published a book called *Who Threw That Coconut?* about his experiences entertaining servicemen throughout the South Pacific.

Some of Colonna's movie appearances were in *Rosalie* (1937) with Eleanor Powell,** *College Swing* (1939) with Burns and Allen, *Road to Singapore* (1940), *Sis Hopkins* (1941) with Judy Canova,* *Atlantic City* (1944) with Constance Moore (married to an agent and living in Beverly Hills), *It's in the Bag* (1945) with Jack Benny and Fred Allen, *Road to Rio* (1947), and *Andy Hardy Comes Home* (1958).

His bellowed singing was recorded in renditions of "Sweet Adeline" and "Down by the Old Mill Stream," both of which sold very well.

By the fifties Jerry was appearing more and more on his own. He played London's Palace Theatre, toured the British Isles in 1956, and made a number of guest appearances on television and radio. In the early sixties he was seen on television's *Super Circus* with ringmaster Claude Kirchner (living in Greenwich, Connecticut).

In August 1966 Jerry Colonna suffered a serious stroke and spent nearly two years recovering in hospitals and then in the Motion Picture Country House in Woodland Hills, California. In 1969 he felt well enough to go with Bob Hope to Vietnam for the comic's annual Christmas show. His appearances were brief but greatly appreciated by the troops.

Interviewed in his Sherman Oaks home recently, he said he was by no means retired and had every intention of resuming his career full time when his health permitted. He is somewhat annoyed when fans ask where he has been and points out that he was seen in a short bit on one of Hope's television shows in 1970. They have no trouble recognizing him: the walrus moustache, which many thought was a paste-on, is as big and as full and ridiculous as ever.

Still clowning. *UPI*

Their first birthday party, 1935, which broke front pages throughout North America.

THE DIONNE QUINTUPLETS

The world's most famous quintuplets were born on a small farm near Callander, Ontario, Canada, on May 28, 1934, in the depths of the depression. Two of the babies were delivered by a midwife before the doctor, Allan Roy Defoe, arrived. Defoe, who shared the quints' fame, presided at the birth of the other three girls and then set to work keeping the children alive in the small frame farmhouse. The coal stove had to be stoked day and night, and since there was no incubator, he used heated bricks and hot-water bottles around the meat basket in which they lay fighting for life. Defoe prescribed a formula of cow's milk, water, corn syrup, and rum (because it was cheaper than brandy) for the children.

The babies' father at first had not intended to call a doctor because of the expense. Now he wondered how he could ever pay for the girls' delivery and support. Three days later he signed a contract to exhibit them at the Chicago World's Fair in return for 23 percent of the admissions. Another 7 percent was to go to the local priest who negotiated the deal. Defoe did not object, thinking the children would not survive anyway. Mrs. Dionne, who had children before and after the quints' birth, at first was embarrassed by the multiple birth, fearing that the press would think of it more as a litter. "They'll call us pigs," she said.

But now the miracle birth was on its way to becoming "North America's No. 1 Peepshow." Canada's prime minister, appalled by the tastelessness, including plans for a souvenir shop, vaudeville tour, and movie contracts, stepped in and made the infants wards of the state.

Nearly overnight the Dionne farm was transformed into a complex of buildings. A large house was built for the parents and their other children, while the quints had a special house with round-the-clock nurses and nuns, and a playground arranged to permit paying visitors to watch the girls.

The girls starred in movies about themselves, *Reunion* (1936) and *The Country Doctor* (1936); Dr. Defoe wrote books and gave endorsements; and Mr. and Mrs. Dionne appeared on a vaudeville circuit with film clips of their babies. Over one thousand tourists a month came to view the children at their farm, and Mr. Dionne's souvenir shop did a brisk business. The local service station named a pump for each girl. The sale of the babies' exclusive photographs to a news service and the franchising of Dionne dolls, spoons, coloring books, and so on around the world brought in a fortune.

When the girls were sent away to a Catholic boarding school, their parents resented the nuns no less than they had resented Dr. Defoe and the nurses. But on their return to their parents' house, which the money from the girls' exploitation purchased and supported, the quints were made to feel like intruders. They were always given the heaviest chores and were led to believe that money was scarce. Not until they had left home in their late teens did they realize that not only was there plenty of money, but that it was all rightfully theirs.

Three months after her twentieth birthday, Emilie, who had become a nun, suffocated during an epileptic seizure. Yvonne has made three unsuccessful attempts to adapt to convent life. She now lives alone in an apartment on the slopes of Mount Royal in Montreal and is an art student at the university there. Annette is married to Germain Allard, a branch manager of a finance company. They reside with their three sons in Saint Bruno, near Montreal. Cecile also married, and had twin boys, but fifteen months later one died. Later she obtained a divorce. Marie, in 1969—three years after she separated from her husband, a government clerk—placed her two daughters in a home operated by Catholic sisters. She had been under psychiatric care when her body was found in February 1970 in her Montreal apartment. Her funeral was the first family reunion in many years.

The girls who once accounted for one-fifth—$25 million—of Canada's tourism, seldom see their parents, who still live on the farm in Callander. Nor have the Dionnes seen all of their grandchildren. Although the girls have an income from a trust fund of over two hundred fifty thousand dollars each, their lives are very quiet, and they are considered "painfully shy."

Standing at the foot of Marie Dionne Houle's casket several months ago are (left to right) Yvonne, Annette, estranged husband Florian Houle, and Cecile, alongside Mr. and Mrs. Oliva Dionne, the quints' parents. Directly in front of the three girls are Monique, seven, and Emilie, nine, Marie's daughters. *UPI*

Slick and sleek in 1935 for Paramount.

GEORGE RAFT

Hollywood's tough guy, born in 1895 in Manhattan's Hell's Kitchen, was of German, Italian, and Dutch parentage, and desperately poor. George was at times a mover's helper, a driver for gangster Owney Madden, a prizefighter, and a dancer. He left home at twelve and though he had very little education, hanging around speakeasies he became an excellent ballroom dancer. For a while George worked for "Texas" Guinan at her El Fey Club.

Little is known of his first marriage except that it was to an older woman who bore him a son, and in 1916 he married actress Grayce Mulrooney. But the most influential woman in his life was Virginia Peine, who divorced her wealthy husband to live with George in a large home he had built for her. Virginia taught him something about dress and poise until he left her for Norma Shearer * and she married the late Quentin Reynolds. After that it was Betty Grable. All Hollywood assumed that George and Betty would marry but their torrid five-year affair ended in 1943 when she married Harry James. Not marrying Grable was a mistake he admits to today.

After appearing on Broadway in such shows as *Gay Paree* (1925) and *Palm Beach Nights* (1926), he went to Hollywood where at first he played small rolls such as in *Quick Millions* (1931) with Sally Eilers (retired and living in Beverly Hills next to Rock Hudson). It was with Paul Muni in *Scarface* (1932) that he really clicked, projecting the epitome of "cool" by repetitiously flipping a coin. Comedians have for years imitated him flipping a coin but he repeated the performance only years later parodying himself in Jerry Lewis's *The Bellboy* (1960). George's roles were not restricted to sinister types but he was always in complete command, even as a convict. Among his some hundred pictures were *Night After Night* (1932) which introduced Mae West to movies, *Bolero* (1934) when he and Carole Lombard started a national tango craze, *Rumba* (1935), *Each Dawn I Die* (1939), *The House Across the Bay* (1940), *Manpower* (1941), *Broadway* (1942), *Nob Hill* (1945), *Johnny Allegro* (1949), *Around the World in 80 Days* (1956), *Some Like It Hot* (1959), and *Rififi in Panama* (1966).

At his height, George made over two hundred thousand dollars annually, but he was very generous with his women and was a compulsive gambler. An irreversible downturn began in 1955. Because of his known association with gamblers and racketeers, the New York Tax Commission refused him permission to buy an interest in the Flamingo. That year he lost one hundred thousand dollars with his ill-fated television series, *I Am the Law,* in which the played a cop. In 1959 his Havana gambling casino (he was a partner) was closed by Fidel Castro, without compensation, and five years later *The George Raft Story,* which starred Ray Danton, flopped.

A year later he appeared for sentencing before a federal judge for income tax evasion. Pleas for clemency from Frank Sinatra, Bob Hope, Red Skelton, Bing Crosby, Jimmy Durante, and Lucille Ball moved the judge to limit the sentence to a fine of twenty-five hundred dollars and a suspended sentence. But as the tears rolled, as he sobbed out his public apology for the television cameras, the tough-guy image was gone forever.

Several months later he was the front man and manager of a posh London gambling club in Berkeley Square. By 1968 though, British authorities left no doubt that George and his associates were unwanted, and he returned to Hollywood to file for Social Security benefits. His Benedict Canyon house and furnishings were auctioned for $63,400, most of it going to his creditors.

George, whose old friends avoid him, is now a grandfather, and survives his nine brothers and sister. He says he has not gambled since he lost sixty-five thousand dollars one night twenty-five years ago. But he is still a natty dresser, and makes an occasional nightclub appearance. The major part of his income these days derives from an Alka-Seltzer commercial in which he plays a convict who starts a riot. It is one of the season's best.

When the State of New Jersey held an investigation of gambling in 1970, Raft was called and was provided with a perfect setting to exhibit his new image—no longer important enough in gambling circles to give any pertinent testimony. The public saw an old man with thin, gray hair, George Raft—loser.

The image dies hard, as seen recently in a Hollywood nightclub. *UPI*

With brother Lee (left) signing autographs on a personal appearance in Indianapolis, Indiana, 1955.

GEORGE LIBERACE

The flamboyant pianist's brother and former partner was born in Menasha, Wisconsin, in 1911. His brother Lee was born eight years later, and they have a sister, Ann, the eldest. Their father, Salvatore, an Italian-born musician who specialized in the French horn, was George's first music teacher. George excelled at the violin, and began in show business playing at Toy's Oriental Restaurant in Milwaukee, followed by appearances at the local Palace and Riverside theatres and then the Milwaukee Philharmonic. For several years he toured the country playing with the bands of Orrin Tucker, Anson Weeks, and Lang Thompson.

Success came to George in 1952 when brother Lee's first television series began to catch on. (Lee's real name is Wladziu Valentino Liberace, shortened to Liberace for business and Lee for friends.) George conducted the orchestra backing Lee, or Liberace, and Liberace incorporated into his act constant references to his mother and "my brother George," which he delivered in his now-famous distinct manner of speech. George was usually in white tie and tails, but seemed diminished next to his brother's dramatic sequin-and-rhinestone ensembles. For five straight years at state fairs, Las Vegas, and television the brothers were one of the top-paid attractions in the business. In 1954 alone their syndicated show was seen in 192 markets throughout the country. Their audiences would never miss a program, though many of them considered the pair one of the funniest comedy acts ever. Of course, there were those who thought they lacked any talent whatsoever, and it was mostly the older women who filled the arenas and theatres wherever the brothers appeared. The ladies seemed especially pleased when Mother Liberace appeared on the show from time to time, and they cheered the boys' constant mention of her. These matrons poured into the movie theatres to see the boys' one film, *Sincerely Yours* (1955), but there were not enough ladies to make it a success.

Few acts took more criticism or ridicule from the press. Music critics were particularly contemptuous of Lee's piano and George's violin. But the brothers would merely repeat Lee's famous remark, "crying all the way to the bank."

In 1957, a mutual jealousy, which friends say existed from the beginning in Milwaukee, came to a head, and George left the act. Letters flooded the network, begging George to return. Most of the correspondence was somewhat reserved in tone compared with Mother Liberace's public utterances. She threatened not to speak to either until they reunited, and blamed the breakup on the "hillbillies and freeloaders" George was seeing. It was all in vain. The brothers have yet to associate professionally.

George first went into the frozen-pizza business, which proved unprofitable, and is now franchising Mr. Turkey (turkey take-out dinners at $1.20) and Mr. Ed restaurants throughout California.

George's wife of four years, Evdora Albrecht, provided him with two step-children, Edward and Donna, both married. Though George is on the road a great deal of the time, he maintains an office in Beverly Hills under the corporate name Music by George that solicits unpublished songs for publication. George is still a performer though. His twenty-five-thousand-dollar violin cum orchestra was heard not long ago in such exclusive spots as Detroit's Hotel Pontchartrain, Reno's Ponderosa, and San Diego's New Town and Country.

Polish-born Mother Liberace, who lives in Hollywood while Father Liberace lives in San Francisco, has never really forgiven the boys for parting, friends say.

Maestro Liberace as he appears today.

Daughter "Lollie Baby" getting a generous dose of Mother Stella love, 1944. *NBC Radio*

STELLA DALLAS: Ann Elstner

"We give you now . . . Stella Dallas . . . a continuation on the air of the true-to-life story of mother love and sacrifice, in which Stella Dallas saw her own beloved daughter Laurel marry into wealth and society and, realizing the differences in their tastes and worlds, went out of Laurel's life." It was late afternoon in most areas of the country when Frank Gallup spoke those lines to millions of radio listeners. Behind him was the theme "How Can I Leave Thee?" played on the studio organ. Women throughout North America were ready for another fifteen minutes with one of fiction's most put-upon women—Stella Dallas.

The first broadcast was on October 25, 1937. Ann Elstner was the radio Stella, which came after the movies based on Olive Higgins Prouty's successful book. She auditioned along with twenty-five other actresses for the role, and played it on NBC Radio for over eighteen years without ever having read the book or seen either of two movie versions. After it was all over and she saw the Barbara Stanwyck picture, she left the theatre sobbing. The earlier film had starred Belle Bennett (Stella), Ronald Colman (Stella's husband), and featured Lois Moran and Douglas Fairbanks, Jr. Actors who worked with Ann on the radio series say that she took the part very seriously, as well as some of the absurd episodes that picked up where the book and movie left off. Once she was supposed to be stranded in a submarine at the bottom of the Suez Canal. Then she braved a sandstorm in the Sahara on her way to rescue her daughter from a harem. In the original version, "Lollie Baby," or Laurel Dallas Grosvenor, had lost her baby. Her mother, who had dropped out of her daughter's life because of the embarrassment of her own background and education, came to her aid. After many twists and turns, it ended with Stella—who never stopped loving her divorced-and-remarried husband, Stephen Dallas—standing at Stephen's side at the funeral of the second Mrs. Dallas. "The world was against Stella," Ann Elstner said only recently. The character was written and played as a common but good-hearted woman without pretensions and obsessed with love for Lollie Baby, played by Vivian Smollen. (Miss Smollen was also for many years the title character of *Our Gal Sunday* on CBS. She lives in Manhattan's East Nineties in the same building with Mary Jane Higby, radio's Nora Drake.) For all the devotion lavished on Lollie, all Stella ever received in return was a set of three pocket handkerchiefs one Christmas!

Stella's best and at times only friend was Minnie Grady, played by Grace Valentine. Others who appeared on the series before they became famous in movies were MacDonald Carey, Ed Begley, Frank Lovejoy, and Raymond Edward Johnson (now retired and in ill health in Middle Springs, Vermont), who was Raymond, the host of *Inner Sanctum.*

Like so many of the soap operas, Stella was produced by Frank and Anne Hummet. It was so popular that when the network announced it would be canceled, the late Cole Porter, a daily listener, enlisted the aid of Lady Mendl and Elsa Maxwell in flooding NBC with protests.

During the program's run, Ann Elstner opened her Stella Dallas' Rivers Edge Restaurant on the banks of the Delaware River in Lambertville, New Jersey, a stone's throw from Bucks County. Few who venture into those parts remain unaware of the establishment; the highways bristle with signs announcing it, proclaiming Stella Dallas herself as proprietress. Ann—a strong right-winger—and her husband, Jack Mathews—a former FBI agent—are around most of the time to greet old fans, including many men and women in their early thirties who listened to her while home sick from school. Said a fellow actor when told that many of the older customers believe Stella was a real person and that Ann Elstner is she: "That wouldn't surprise Ann. I think most of the time she believes it herself."

Stella with Richard Lamparski in Manhattan's Paley Park. *Diana Keyt*

Under contract to Twentieth Century-Fox, 1938.

JACK HALEY

The light film-and-stage comedian of the thirties and forties was born in Boston, Massachusetts, in 1902. His was a poor Irish-Catholic family, and no one he knew was connected with show business. But after Jack saw a comic in a Christmas benefit for underprivileged children, he decided to be a famous funny man, with lots of money. Within forty years, he managed both.

He made his debut at the age of six, singing a song called "Leapfrog Jump" in a Catholic church play. After graduating from Dwight Grammar School, he bummed around at a number of odd jobs. First he worked in a New York law office for $3.50 a week. Then he went to Philadelphia, where he made as much as $60 weekly as a song plugger in vaudeville houses. He used a pointer and encouraged audiences to sing along with him. His first act was with six girls. Within six months he was booked into the Palace Theatre in New York, minus the girls. His partner was Charlie Crofts and their act was called Crofts and Haley. Jack describes it as "the Martin and Lewis of our day." He also worked with Benny Rubin (who lives alone in Hollywood, writing television scripts) a former best friend until a falling-out two years ago. Jack's most successful liaison, professionally and privately, was with a girl named Florence MacFadden on an act not unlike "Burns and Allen." They have been husband and wife forty-seven years.

Jack had his first big break in 1929 when he introduced the song "Button Up Your Overcoat" in the hit musical *Follow Through*. In 1930, he did the screen version with Zelma O'Neal, both in secondary leads, and Buddy Rogers and the late Nancy Carroll, the stars. The film set the pattern for most of Jack's movie work: he never got the girl unless she was a Patsy Kelly or Joan Davis. In 1932 he was back on Broadway in *Take a Chance* with Ethel Merman and the late Olsen and Johnson.

Among his some fifty films were *Sitting Pretty* (1933) with Jack Oakie,**

Coronado (1935) with Johnny Downs (the emcee of a daily television show in San Diego, California), *Wake Up and Live* (1937) with Alice Faye, *Alexander's Ragtime Band* (1938), *Rebecca of Sunnybrook Farm* (1938) with Shirley Temple, *The Wizard of Oz* (1939), and *George White's Scandals* (1945).

Undoubtedly, Jack remains best remembered for *The Wizard of Oz*, the motion-picture classic that "at the time . . . just seemed like another movie," in which he played the Tin Man and Hickory.

He was in the stage version of the musical *Higher and Higher* (1940), repeated his role for the movie in 1943, starred on Broadway in *Show Time* (1942) with the late Ella Logan, and followed with *Inside U.S.A.* (1948) with Bea Lillie, which they also took on the road. From then on, Jack devoted himself to his real estate investments and cattle raising.

However, in 1969 he was directed by Jack, Jr. in *Norwood* playing Joe Namath's father. Jack was reluctant to do it but it was Junior's first movie and he wanted his father in it for good luck. He also has a daughter, Gloria, who has given him two grandchildren.

Jack has little interest in working again, although as a favor to his old friend Jackie Gleason he did a 1969 guest shot on his television show. He is at his office every day to check on his Maderna Acres development, other investments, and new projects.

Jack's Beverly Hills home occupies a corner lot just off Sunset Boulevard which includes among other autos a Cadillac and a Rolls-Royce.

His ultramodern house is the scene of frequent parties for his many old friends, among them Walter O'Keefe, Charlie Ruggles, Charles Correll * (of *Amos 'n' Andy* fame), and Norman Frescott ("The Great Frescott" of vaudeville days, now retired and living with his wife Benjie in Studio City).

At home with Flo in Beverly Hills. *Diana Keyt*

In the *Ziegfeld Follies of 1919*.

RAY DOOLEY

The Infant Terrible, the title by which she was known to audiences for over two decades, was born on October 30, 1896, in Glasgow, Scotland. Her father was a clown well known in circuses throughout Great Britain. The Dooleys migrated to the United States when Ray, whose real name is Rachel Rice Dooley, was still quite young. During her childhood she was part of an act billed as "The Four Dooleys" that enjoyed great popularity on the vaudeville circuits.

Ray made her debut as a single when she was only ten years old playing an even younger little girl. She was a huge success singing "I'm Afraid of the Great Big Moon." None of the Dooleys would ever make it as big as Ray, although her brother Gordon was to play with her in the *Earl Carroll Vanities*. The other two Dooleys were William and Johnny.

By 1910 she was billed as "Ray Dooley and the Metropolitan Minstrels." In 1914 Ray appeared in a patriotic show written by Irving Berlin (living quietly in his mansion on New York City's Beekman Place) especially to bolster morale among the doughboys in World War I. The show was called *Yip, Yip, Yaphank* and she played the role of Mandy.

Miss Dooley was a special favorite of W. C. Fields, with whom she worked in four Broadway hits and one flop. The latter was when Flo Ziegfeld starred them in *Comic Supplement* in 1925. The show closed in Washington, D.C., before it reached New York. The successes they did together were *Ziegfeld Follies* of 1920, *Ziegfeld Follies* of 1921, *Ziegfeld Follies* of 1925, and *Earl Carroll Vanities* of 1928.

Some of her other hits were *No Foolin'* (1926) with Paulette Goddard,* *Honeymoon Lane* (1926) which introduced Kate Smith to Broadway, *Sidewalks of New York* (1927), and *Thumbs Up* (1934) with Bobby Clark and Sheila Barrett, the monologist (living in a Manhattan hotel). The last three were presented by her producer-author-actor husband, Eddie Dowling.* She was also in his film *Honeymoon Lane* (1931).

Ray Dooley was what is called in show business a performer's performer. She was original, spontaneous, and extremely funny. In many of her appearances she impersonated a baby with a ferocious disposition. Her trademarks in these skits were a baby's bonnet and a nippled bottle which often was used as a weapon. After Ray retired soon after giving birth to a daughter, Mary Maxine, in 1937, Fanny Brice reactivated her career with a similar act she called "Baby Snooks." In spite of her direct steal, the two remained friends until Miss Brice died. Ray had wished her old friend well with the role.

Ray's only appearance on Broadway after *Thumbs Up* was in 1948 when she was seen in the one-act *Home Life of a Buffalo,* which was part of *Hope Is the Thing with Feathers,* produced by her husband.

The comedienne seldom leaves her East Hampton, Long Island, home except to attend mass or to baby-sit for her grandchildren. The Dowlings are devout Roman Catholics. Eddie Dowling, her husband of over fifty years, is presently putting together a television special on her life in the theatre. Always extremely shy, Ray has avoided public appearances and interviews since her only son Edward John, born in 1914, was killed several years ago in Argentina while on assignment as a reporter for Time-Life.

Ray and Eddie near their East Hampton, Long Island, home. *Peaches Poland*

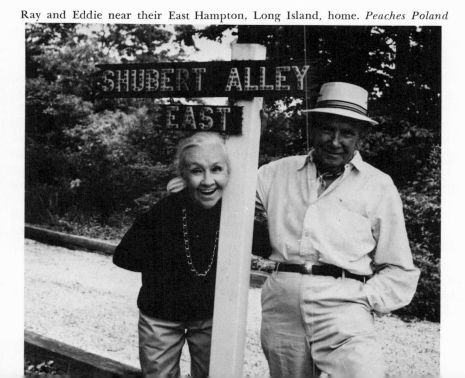

A 1948 publicity portrait from RKO Studios.

HOAGY CARMICHAEL

The composer-singer-actor was born in Bloomington, Indiana, on November 22, 1899. His real name is Hoagland Howard Carmichael. Hoagy learned to play the piano from his mother, who used to entertain the neighborhood with mini-concerts of ragtime. Later, while attending law school at the University of Indiana, he paid his tuition with what he made from a three-piece orchestra he led. Even while in school, his "Riverboat Shuffle" was published, and the late Paul Whiteman performed Hoagy's "Washboard Blues." But when he received his bachelor of law degree in 1926, Carmichael was determined to be an attorney, not a songwriter.

He attempted to set up a law practice in Florida but when success was not immediately forthcoming he joined Jean Goldkette's Orchestra. He was with Goldkette only a few months before he left to head his own group in Indianapolis. When that didn't work out, he began arranging music in Tin Pan Alley in New York City.

In 1927 Hoagy made his first records—for the Gennett label, leading an orchestra that included Jimmy and Tommy Dorsey. Another recording group he led included Benny Goodman and Bix Beiderbecke. In the later twenties Hoagy took part in some of the first integrated recording sessions.

Hoagy's idol and closest friend was Bix Beiderbecke. He died in 1931 at the age of twenty-nine, the year Carmichael published his biggest hit, "Star Dust." He had no idea what the title meant but he liked the sound of the words. The lyrics were written by Mitchell Parish. To this day it remains a standard tune included in the repertoire of nearly every pianist, singer, and orchestra in the country.

Hoagy not only scored and wrote songs for movies but also appeared in a number of them. His most impressive role was the piano player in *To Have and Have Not* (1944) with Humphrey Bogart and Lauren Bacall. Some of his others were *Johnny Angel* (1945), *Canyon Passage* (1946), *The Best Years of Our Lives* (1946), and *Young Man with a Horn* (1950), the biography of Beiderbecke. When he wasn't playing himself Carmichael was the loveable loser, an image he often conveys to those who do not know him well. Although his manner is somewhat lethargic, Hoagy does not lack ambition and energy, or success. His autobiography, *Washboard Blues,* was published in 1947.

Some of his past hits are "Georgia on My Mind," "Hong Kong Blues," "Little Old Lady," "Lazy Bones," "Lazy River," "I Get Along Without You Very Well," "Old Rocking Chair," and "Skylark." In 1946 his "Ole Buttermilk Sky" was nominated for the best song of the year. He sang it in *Canyon Passage.* In 1951 he shared the Oscar for "In the Cool, Cool, Cool of the Evening" with lyricist Johnny Mercer. The song was sung by Bing Crosby and Jane Wyman in *Here Comes the Groom.*

He was a regular guest on network variety shows during the forties and had his own program during the 1946–1947 season. In 1951 he headlined the show at London's Palladium which he was as much the personality and singer as he was the composer. In the summer of 1953 Carmichael hosted the *Saturday Night Revue,* the ninety-minute replacement for the *Show of Shows.* For the most part it was panned by critics. During the 1960–1961 season he had a running part in the television western series *Laramie.*

Hoagy's one marriage, to Ruth Meinardi, ended after nineteen years in a 1955 divorce. They have two boys, Randy, who is pursuing a career as a pianist and composer, and Bix, who is with a brokerage house.

The gravel-voiced entertainer still receives a huge income from song royalties as well as from his investments in Palm Springs and Las Vegas real estate. He maintains a penthouse overlooking the Sunset Strip in Hollywood and a $143,000 home across from the Thunderbird golf course in Palm Springs. Hoagy is an avid golfer and a frequent visitor to Las Vegas, where he attends openings of his friends.

Although he has not had a hit in some time, the tunesmith continues to work at his craft. While his sound is still greatly appreciated by many, Carmichael's songs no longer attract young people. In 1967 Hoagy released a composition, "From Nikki's Garden," but it never made the charts or juke boxes. However, he is still very much in evidence among the big names in the music world on the West Coast even if they don't sing his new songs.

On a visit to the Desert Inn on his seventieth birthday. *Wide World*

In an ensemble that was the height of chic in 1941.

DOLORES DEL RIO

The Latin movie beauty was born Lolita Dolores Martinez Asunsolo Lopez Negrette in Durango, Mexico, on August 3, 1905. She lived in Durango on a huge family-owned ranch until she was four years old. Her father, a banker, was forced to flee with his wife and daughter to Mexico City to escape the revolutionary Pancho Villa.

Dolores was educated in Mexico's capital city at the Convent of Saint Joseph and, as was the custom among the class-conscious rich, was presented to the king and queen of Spain while on a European trip in 1919.

Two years later Dolores married Jamie Del Rio, an attorney eighteen years her senior. Soon after, Hollywood director Edwin Carewe while visiting saw her dancing at a home party and offered her a chance to act in his film *Joanna* (1925). It was unheard of for a girl of her background to consider a theatrical career, but her mother and husband felt it might be fun. Only Dolores took the idea seriously. She was brokenhearted when most of her footage was edited out of her first two pictures. She was treated much better in the next two: *Whole Town's Talking* (1926) and *Pals First* (1926). Then she won the role of Charmaine in the blockbuster *What Price Glory* (1926). Although it was a man's picture she did not go unnoticed. Even in an industry and city steeped in glamour and beauty Dolores Del Rio was a standout. She appeared with the late Rod La Rocque in *Resurrection* (1927).

By the time she appeared in the title role in *Ramona* (1928) she had succeeded in becoming an important star while at the same time her marriage had come apart and her director had fallen in love with her. Carewe's wife was suing him for divorce, and Hollywood expected him to marry Dolores. But before she could obtain a divorce from Del Rio he died suddenly. Many felt Del Rio's spirit had been broken by his role as Dolores Del Rio's husband. But it was all academic. Dolores made *Evangeline* (1929) with Carewe and then broke with him completely.

In talkies, Dolores's weakness as an actress was somewhat more obvious but she more than made up for that shortcoming with her beauty and voice, which was also heard in song. Some of her American sound pictures were

The Bad One (1930), *Bird of Paradise* (1932), *Flying Down to Rio* (1933), *Wonder Bar* (1934, *In Caliente* (1935) with Wini Shaw (The Lady in Red lives with her husband, a box-office treasurer in Sunnyside, Queens, New York), and *International Settlement* (1938) with June Lang (living with her daughter in North Hollywood, California).

Her ten-year marriage to set designer Cedric Gibbons ended in 1941, whereupon she entered into an affair with Orson Welles. She made *Journey into Fear* (1942) with him as costar and director, but their relationship ended shortly afterward when he married Rita Hayworth. In the next eighteen years Dolores made only one Hollywood film, *The Fugitive* (1947), although she was very active in South American and Mexican productions. In 1960 she played Elvis Presley's mother in *Flaming Star*. Since her return to Hollywood she has appeared several times on such television series as *Marcus Welby, M.D.* and in feature films *Cheyenne Autumn* (1964) and *More Than a Miracle* (1967).

Dolores Del Rio travels a great deal of the time and is still a big star in Mexico, where she won four Arieles (their Oscars), in Spain, where she picked up Spain's Oscar, the Quixote, and in South America where she also appears on the stage.

Although her acting skills have improved considerably in the last twenty years, Dolores is best remembered among fans for her dazzling beauty, most of which she has retained to a degree that borders on the uncanny. She is undoubtedly the most beautiful of all the surviving stars of the silent era and takes great care to remain so with strict abstinence from smoking, drinking, and overeating. Several years ago her contemporary Aileen Pringle ** asked her how she could look so young. Dolores answered that she was a Yogi. "We think up!" she told the drinking, smoking, wrinkled Pringle. She reportedly sleeps as much as twelve hours a night.

Since 1959 she has been married to Lewis Riley, an American who produces in Latin-American countries. Their home is a two hundred-year-old house on a large estate in Coyacán, an exclusive suburb of Mexico City surrounded by lush gardens and containing a collection of pre-Columbian art.

On a recent trip to New York City. *Jon Virzi*

In 1938, a featured singer on Jack Benny's radio program.

KENNY BAKER

The popular tenor of the 1930s and 1940s was born Kenneth Lawrence Baker in Monrovia, California, in 1912. He attended high school and entered junior college in Long Beach, California, with the intention of becoming a concert violinist. But soon after he joined the glee club, his voice became the focal point of his ambition. In order to pay for voice lessons Kenny worked as a laborer on the Boulder Dam, as a farmhand in Mexico, and as a mover for a Los Angeles furniture store.

Paying jobs began in 1930 when he made nineteen-dollar-a-week singing commercials on a Long Beach radio station, a position that lasted twenty weeks. Then he joined a quartet of students from the California Christian College.

Kenny's big break came in 1933 when he entered a national contest being conducted by the Texaco dealers. Kenny, along with scores of other contestants from around the country, sang on the network radio program *Going Places*. The program emanated live from the Coconut Grove in Los Angeles and featured the Eddy Duchin Orchestra, at the time one of the most popular groups in the country. The exposure alone got Kenny tempting offers to sing in clubs but, when he was picked as the favorite, the Hollywood studios beckoned.

His first two movies, *Metropolitan* with Lawrence Tibbett and *King of Burlesque,* were released in 1935. They were followed by *Turn Off the Moon* (1937) with Eleanor Whitney (Mrs. Frederick Backer of New York City), *The King and the Chorus Girl* (1937) with Fernand Gravet (active on the stage in Paris), *Goldwyn Follies* (1938) with Helen Jepson (Mrs. Walter Dellera of Orange, New Jersey) and Vera Zorina, *Radio City Revels* (1938) with Jack Oakie ** and the late Bob Burns, *The Mikado* (1939), *The Hit Parade of 1941* (1940) with Frances Langford,** *Doughboys in Ireland* (1943), and *The Harvey Girls* (1946), his last. Kenny also appeared in two

64

Marx Brothers films: *A Day at the Races* (1937) and *At the Circus* (1939). If Kenny ever had a chance to become a big star it was in the film version of *The Mikado,* in which he played the role of Nanki-Poo. The film was well received by critics for its color and Gilbert-and-Sullivan songs, but it did poorly at the box office.

For all the movies he made, Baker's greatest claim to fame at the time came from his appearances each Sunday night as the vocalist on America's most popular radio program, the *Jack Benny Show,* on NBC's Red Network. He appeared in the late 1930s for several seasons until he was replaced by Dennis Day.

In 1943 Baker made an auspicious Broadway debut when he appeared opposite Mary Martin in the smash hit *One Touch of Venus.*

In the early fifties he did some television but the exposure did little for his fading career. In 1956 the Bakers moved to Solvang, California, a small community north of Santa Barbara which was settled originally by immigrant Danes. Most of the shopping district and many of the homes in the town bore the architectural features of a Danish village. As the only celebrity in the charming town, Kenny Baker's house is often pointed out to tourists.

Kenny has been a convert to Christian Science since 1926, and during the past twenty years has devoted considerable time to his church. "There came a time when I desired to be of service to mankind in a different way," he says. "The world is full of entertainments but starved for things of true substance and enduring values."

Baker is also a member of the local Planning Commission and is active in the management of a record company that deals exclusively in sacred music. His voice is heard on a number of its albums. The Baker children, two boys and a girl, have married and now have children of their own. Kenny and his wife, who have been married since 1933, on their front lawn have a large rock lettered Jesus Saves.

Relaxing in Solvang, California. *Jon Virzi*

In 1941.

ANDRÉ EGLEVSKY

The celebrated premier danseur of the 1930s and 1940s was born in Moscow in 1917. His cossack father was a colonel in the czarist army. Shortly after André's birth, his mother, Zoe Obranoff Eglevsky, disguised herself and fled with him and his sister to Constantinople, and then to Bulgaria. By the time the three settled in a small fishing village near Nice in the south of France, the hardships of travel and scarcity of food had left André with a puny physique and dangerously weakened lungs. Then after the child's serious bout with pneumonia Madame Eglevsky decided that the strict discipline of ballet training would be good for her son.

He was enrolled at the age of seven with a Madame Maria Nevelska, who within a week proclaimed that the boy would or could have a great future. She arranged for an audition with Michael Fokine in Paris. Fokine, who had enormous influence in the dance world, was so taken with the youngster's talent that he offered to adopt him. Madame Eglevsky was unenthusiastic about the adoption but agreed that her son's career should be guided by the impressario. André was taught by Alexander Volinine, who had been a partner of the legendary Pavlova, Matilde Vachessinska, and Lubov Egorova in Paris. Later, in London, André trained under Nicolas Legat. Leonide Massine after watching the fourteen-year-old André in class one day arranged for him to join the Corps de Ballet of the Ballet de Monte Carlo. Within a very short time, in tours of the Continent and North Africa, Eglevsky was dancing leads in *Les Sylphides* and *Swan Lake,* to glowing notices.

For a boy whose first memories of dance were those of loathing, he did extremely well. He recalls that his mother bribed him with ice cream in return for the time spent in class. Soon, however, the only incentive he needed was praise from Madame Nevelska and his classmates, and his rapid progress amazed them. He admits today that it was the applause that came shortly after that forged his life-long addiction to the art of the dance. And once he developed the body and skill of a great dancer, he acquired the manner and temperament of a star.

André conveyed a feeling of great power in his dancing and although he performed with nearly every prima ballerina of the time, was never overshadowed. Socially and professionally, however, he stressed his masculinity in private conversations and in interviews until it is as embarrassing as it is unconvincing. In 1934, when he first wore tights onstage in the United States, in Saint Louis, the audience, which then was used to seeing its male dancers in trousers, laughed out loud.

In 1938, he surprised contemporaries by ending a torrid affair with a ballerina to marry another dancer, Leda Anchutin, of Tartar descent, and a year later he became a United States citizen. The Russian Orthodox couple have three children.

Eglevsky danced with the Ballet Theatre from 1942 to 1946 and then with the Marquis de Cuevas Company from 1948 to 1951, when he joined the New York City Ballet under Balanchine. His own Eglevsky Ballet Company has been presented as part of the Balanchine performances.

The only public records of his art are in a short he made for Warner Brothers and in the film *Limelight* (1952) in the ballet sequence. When producer-star Charlie Chaplin's representative first approached Eglevsky, he thought it was a joke: as a boy, André's heroes were not great dancers but Rudolph Valentino and Chaplin, and the association proved to be one of the happiest periods of his career.

Eglevsky—whose naturally high-pitched voice trembles at any reference to any mention of the enormously wealthy older men who sponsored him during the early years of his career—is retired for about a decade now. He teaches dance several days a week at the New York City Ballet studios and operates his own dancing school near his home in Massapequa, Long Island. He says he would much prefer to direct a school sponsored by the government, as it is done in many European countries. He resents the paper work and financial matters, although he admits that having a name puts him in a much better position to deal with mothers, who are the despair of most ballet masters.

With Richard Lamparski at WBAI–FM studios, New York. *Michael Knowles*

Just before the accident in 1925 that ended her career.

ANNA Q. NILSSON

The early silent star whose career came to a tragic, abrupt end was born Anna Querentia Nilsson in Ystad, Sweden, in 1890. She was still in her early teens when a neighbor, just returned from a trip to the United States, came by the Nilsson home for a visit. She wore a hat made of ostrich plumes. "I'd never seen anything so beautiful in my life as that hat," recalls Anna, "and I decided that America was the place for me."

Anna had worked and saved some money and, after much persuasion, her parents permitted her to go to New York with another girl from Ystad but with the promise that she would stay with family friends there.

Upon her arrival in 1907, Anna worked as a nursemaid and took English lessons so she could get a better job. One day when she stopped in front of Carnegie Hall to check on an address, the artist Carol Bickwith saw her and asked if she would pose for him. Her hosts were horrified when they heard about it and threatened to write to her parents. But Anna leaped at the opportunity. Soon she was known as the Stanlow Poster Girl, and she began to pose for photographers as well. During this period, she made strong friendships with two other girls who were soon to be movie stars, the late Alice Joyce and Mabel Normand.

One of the photographers who got a job with the Kalem Company, an early producer of movies, recommended Anna as an actress for the one-reeler *Molly Pitcher* (1913), and she stayed with the Kalem Company for five years. She made such pictures as *Barriers Swept Aside* (1915), *Scarlet Road* (1916), *Seven Keys to Baldpate* (1917), *Heart of the Sunset* (1918), and *Way of the Strong* (1919). Some other films were *One Hour Before Dawn* (1920), *In the Heart of a Fool* (1921), *Ponjola* (1923), in which she played a boy, and *Midnight Lovers* (1926), finished in 1925.

Then one day in 1925 she and a friend went riding in the mountains. Just as they approached a stone wall, her horse, frightened by a snake, threw her and she struck the wall. She was carried back to the hotel and the doctor who examined her said that all she needed was rest. After five days in bed the pain in her hip had become so bad that she demanded to be taken to Los Angeles. The doctor, it was later discovered, was a drug addict, and her hip had been shattered. Anne was operated on and spent a year in the hospital but still couldn't walk. She endured still another operation with the same negative results and more long months of recuperation. She decided to return to Sweden to see if the doctors there could help her but was persuaded aboard ship to consult a specialist in Vienna. In Vienna, she was told she would need another operation. She refused and traveled to Stockholm where she was advised to work with a therapist. When she returned to America a year later her friends had a stretcher and nurse waiting at dockside. To their utter amazement Anna walked down the gangplank and has walked perfectly ever since.

By the time she was well, however, talkies were in and she had been off the screen for several years. "At first I was heartbroken that my career was ended but I get over things very quickly," she said recently. Her money had been well invested and she threw herself into a life of charity work, reading, and extensive travel. Several times she was talked into bit parts in sound films such as *World Changes* (1933) and *I Live on Danger* (1942) but confesses that each time she was terrified: "Everything was so different from when I had worked before, and I never had much confidence in myself."

Anna had two brief marriages. The first was in 1916 to G. Coombs, whom she describes as "a darling but also a drunk." In 1923 she married John Gunnerson, "a drunken bum."

Six years ago, no longer active in her charity work or traveling, Anna moved from Beverly Hills to the senior citizen project in Sun City, California, where she is the toast of the town. All her neighbors are old enough to remember her and she is the only film personality there. She sees lots of movies, gardens, and plays bridge a great deal.

Young people today know Miss Nilsson for her cameo role in *Sunset Boulevard* (1950) in which she played cards with Gloria Swanson, the late H. B. Warner, and Buster Keaton. Anna keeps in touch with very few of her screen contemporaries although she was visited by Conrad Nagel just before he died in 1970; Anna starred in his first film.

"I was never very social even when I was a star," she explains. "And when I was, it was always with men. It must be the Swedish in me. I can be alone for weeks on end." Among the mementos in her living room is an autographed picture of Rudolph Valentino signed "To the beautiful blonde Viking."

Valentino's "beautiful blonde Viking" today. *Clifford May*

Heavyweight Champion of the World, 1932. *The Ring*

JACK SHARKEY

The former Heavyweight Champion of the World was born of Lithuanian parents in Binghamton, New York, on October 6, 1902. He left school at the age of twelve and held various jobs until he was old enough to join the navy.

When he entered the service in 1920 he had never worn a pair of boxing gloves nor had he ever been much attracted to athletics. Shortly afterward he got into a losing street brawl with a fellow sailor who he later discovered was the champion of Rhode Island. When he left the navy in 1924 he had fought twenty bouts, impressing his shipmates and himself with his superb defensive skills.

He promptly changed his name, Josef Paul Cuckoschay, to Jack Sharkey, a combination of the names of his two fistic idols, Tom Sharkey and Jack Dempsey. He signed with Boston promoter Johnny Buckley, a partnership that lasted through his professional life.

Jack received one hundred fifty dollars for his first pro fight, in which he knocked out Billy Muldoon in one round. During the next two years he made quite a name for himself by defeating Johnny Risko, Jim Maloney, Jack Renault, and George Godfrey. But it was in 1927 that Sharkey got into the champion contender class: he knocked out Homer Smith, stopped Mike McTigue, and then beat Jim Maloney again by a KO.

On July 21, 1927, Sharkey was matched against Jack Dempsey in Yankee Stadium. It drew boxing history's fourth million-dollar gate and promised the victor a crack at the title held by Gene Tunney.* Although many claimed that Dempsey fouled him, Sharkey was knocked out in the seventh round.

In early 1928 Sharkey was held to a draw by Tom Heeney and then lost a fifteen-round decision to Johnny Risko. These defeats cost him a chance against Tunney, but Sharkey's supreme self-confidence, for which he was noted during his career, saw him through victories over Jack Delaney, Young Stribling, and Tommy Loughran.

After Tunney retired undefeated, Sharkey was pitted against Max Schmeling * on June 12, 1930. The German won on a foul in the fourth round. When the two met again two years and nine days later, Jack brought the heavyweight crown back to the United States by winning a split decision after a full fifteen rounds. To view the match at the Long Island City Bowl, 61,863 fans had paid $432,465 on June 21, 1932.

A little over a year later he defended his title for the first and last time against the late Primo Carnera.* Jack, who weighed in at 201, was knocked out in the sixth round in Long Island City. Later that year, Jack lost decisions to King Levinsky (now selling ties) and Tommy Loughran, and then went into retirement briefly. He devoted all of his time to the tavern he opened in Boston until he tried a comeback in 1935. By this time Jim Braddock * held the title and Jack had to fight Joe Louis, another top challenger, for a shot at it. Jack Sharkey was a very good boxer but he never had a great punch. The Brown Bomber stopped him after one minute and twelve seconds of the third round. The place was Yankee Stadium and the date was August 18, 1936. At age thirty-three Jack hung up his gloves.

Jack's money was saved during his ring career and invested well. Until 1952 he lived in the Chestnut Hill section of Boston, at which time he sold out his business interests and tavern and moved permanently to his summer home in Epping, New Hampshire. He and his wife of forty-six years, the former Dorothy Pike, have three children who have presented them with eighteen grandchildren. Although he considers himself retired, several times a year the Sharkeys travel about the country with the Sportsmen's and Camping Show. One of its biggest draws is the former champion's flycasting exhibition. He also does some occasional refereeing. During the warm weather Jack's favorite pastime is fishing. Colder weather finds him on hunting trips throughout New England.

With Ted Williams (left) during their flycasting match in Boston recently. *UPI*

In 1947, when *My Friend Irma* began on radio.

MARIE WILSON

The dumb but lovable blond was born Katherine Elizabeth Wilson in Anaheim, California, in 1916. When her father and mother were divorced seven months later, her father put eleven thousand dollars in the bank for Marie. When she was twenty years old, Marie convinced her mother that the money should be spent to launch her on a career in movies. The entire sum was turned over to her, and the family promptly moved to Hollywood.

First she took a large house, paying up the rent for a year, bought a new car, a mink coat, canned goods to last for months, and a set of false teeth for her stepfather. Within two weeks she had not only spent all the money but was $1.38 overdrawn at the bank.

Marie went to work in the toy department of a store but was fired after she talked one man out of paying $25 for a teddy bear and giving away merchandise to poor children. She started doing extra work in films and was placed under contract to Warner Bros.

Marie already had been screen-tested at M-G-M but had not been signed. However, after Jack Warner hired her on the strength of it, once he had her at the studio he just didn't know what to do with her. She wanted to do straight parts, although in the test she did a comedy scene. Warner wanted her to be neither funny nor dramatic but sexy. The result was that she appeared briefly in a few pictures such as *Satan Met a Lady* (1936), and the original version of the *Maltese Falcon* (1941), playing Warren William's secretary.

By 1941 her Warner Bros. contract was up. She was offered a part in a production of *Out of the Frying Pan* which was to be produced onstage in San Francisco. But at the same time, Ken Murray wanted her for his *Blackouts*. Since she didn't think either would run for more than a few weeks, Marie chose *Blackouts,* co-produced by Billy Gilbert.** Murray, with whom she had done radio work, felt she could be both sexy and funny. Sample of their routine:

Murray: Where were you born?

Marie: In Anaheim in a grapefruit grove.

Murray: [*leering at her ample cleavage*] Well, that explains a couple of things!

In spite of bad reviews the show ran until 1949 when Murray took it to Broadway, without Marie, where it closed after only fifty-one performances. Marie played 2,332 shows, beginning with a weekly salary of two hundred fifty dollars and ending with one thousand dollars.

In 1947 her *My Friend Irma* series began on radio and was an immediate success with the public, although it ran twenty weeks before CBS was able to sell it. With her well-practiced verbal ingenuousness, Marie was able to project the character of the featherbrained Irma to millions who were unable to see her until the show moved to television in 1952. The late Kathy Lewis was her practical friend for most of the episodes. It went off the network in June 1954 but continued for years in reruns.

Marie has appeared in a number of pilot films that were never sold to television. She was back in *Blackouts* when it was revived in Hollywood for sixteen weeks in 1960 and has played Las Vegas clubs many times. In the early sixties Miss Wilson toured the country as Lorelei Lee in the musical *Gentlemen Prefer Blondes*. She was seriously considered for the film version of *Born Yesterday* but lost out to the late Judy Holliday.

Today she lives in the Outpost section of Hollywood with television producer Bob Fallon, to whom she has been married since 1951. Previously she was married to and divorced from director Nick Grinde and actor-writer Alan Nixon. The Fallons have a teen-age son, Gregson, named for his godfather, attorney Greg Bautzer. From time to time Marie appears around the country in *Born Yesterday*, and in 1969 she played it in Chicago and Saint Louis. Marie's is the voice of Penny the housewife in the television cartoon series *Where's Huddles?* over CBS. She still sees a great deal of Ken Murray and Cy Howard, who created the *Irma* show.

Talking recently about her professional image she said, "It has been very good to me and I'm not complaining, but some day I just wish someone would offer me a different kind of role. My closest friends admit that whenever they tell someone they know me they have to convince them that I'm really not dumb. To tell you the truth I think people are disappointed that I'm not."

At home in Hollywood. *Gary Leavitt*

Henry in 1940. *NBC Radio*

HENRY ALDRICH: Ezra Stone

Once America's most popular teen-ager, Henry began as a character in a hit Broadway play, *What a Life,* in 1938. During the run, Rudy Vallee invited Henry, or Ezra Stone, to do a bit from the play on his radio show. The late Ted Collins heard the program and signed Ezra to do a series of skits about Henry for *The Kate Smith Show.* The skits were written by the play's author, Clifford Goldsmith.

In 1939 the network was looking for a replacement for the *Jack Benny Show* during his summer hiatus and hit on the idea of *Henry Aldrich* as a thirty-minute-weekly series. Collins bet Stone that it wouldn't last the summer. The author was equally pessimistic, having told his agent, "I just can't see how there can be any more to say about that boy." The show lasted until 1953 and had a counterpart on television during the last few years.

Although touted as the life of a typical American boy, the show's audience was made up of very young children and those who could barely remember their teens. Ezra Stone's distinctive voice was his own invention. He had lisped as a child, and while his voice now was perfectly natural, he copied the squeaky, cracking sound of his best friend, Charles Moose. Every Thursday night an audience of between thirty and thirty-five million tuned in to the program that opened with Kay Raft's (now acting in commercials in New York) call: "Hen-reee! Henry Aldrich!" followed by Stone's famous, "Coming, mother!" Sam Aldrich, Henry's father, was played by House Jameson (now retired and living in Newton, Connecticut). Henry's best friend, Homer Brown, was played by Jackie Kelk (now a casting director for a large New York advertising agency).

The original play was made into a movie in 1939 with Jackie Cooper and was followed by a series of features based on *The Aldrich Family* radio program. Though Ezra Stone tested for the series several times, the part of Henry went to Jimmy Lydon (the associate producer of the film *The Learning Tree;* he has been married to the daughter of the acting couple character actor Bernard Nedell, who now resides in Manhattan, and the late Olive Blakeney, who played Mrs. Aldrich in the series).

Stone was discontented with his role as an actor even when the program was at its height. He had been in *Brother Rat* on stage for two seasons and *Three Men on a Horse* for one season. "It was my misfortune to be in nothing but hits," he said in a recent interview. "Misfortune because I was bored by the repetition. I kept adding to my parts, trying to get more laughs. Finally my old drama teacher told me one day that I simply was not temperamentally suited to be an actor. He was right."

Ezra began directing. As early as 1939 he had directed Milton Berle in *See My Lawyer* on Broadway. When the *Aldrich* series ended in 1953, he began in earnest directing television and radio. Ezra has since directed for television *Julia, The Debbie Reynolds Show,* and several segments of *The Flying Nun* to add to his earlier directorial credits: *The Munsters, Petticoat Junction,* and *Lost in Space.* In addition, Ezra is in charge of films and conventions for IBM.

He and his wife, the former actress Sara Seeger, divide their time between their homes in the Hollywood hills and a farm in Bucks County, Pennsylvania. Their daughter Francine is the second female president in the history of the Harvard Drama Club. Their son Josef runs the farm and flies his own plane.

Not long ago, the Hollywood Bowl was taken over for one night in a salute to the golden days of radio. Among the many veterans of the medium who performed in songs and skits from their heyday were Ezra Stone and House Jameson in a sketch written especially for the evening by Clifford Goldsmith and directed by their old director Harry Ackerman (now one of television's most successful producers).

Now a director, at his desk in Hollywood. *Clifford May*

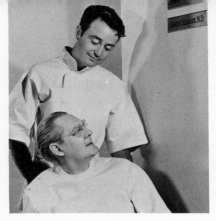

With Lionel Barrymore in a scene from their *Dr. Kildare* series.

LEW AYRES

The movie matinee idol who became America's first well-known conscientious objector was born Lewis Fredrick Ayres III in 1908 in Minneapolis. His parents were divorced when he was four, and he went to live with his grandmother. At fifteen his mother and stepfather took Lew with them to live in San Diego. At one point he left high school to play saxophone and guitar with the Henry Halstead and Ray West bands. Later he enrolled in the University of Arizona's School of Medicine but left after a short time.

It was at a tea dance that a movie executive spotted him gliding across the floor with Lily Damita (now retired and living in Miami Beach, Florida) and signed him to a six-month contract with Pathé. He made one film for them, *The Sophomore* (1929), and then went to M-G-M, where he made the silent *The Kiss* opposite Greta Garbo.

Carl Laemmle, Jr., was producing *All Quiet on the Western Front* (1930) and Paul Bern, an influential movie executive who later married Jean Harlow, suggested Ayres for the lead. In his interview with the director Lew seemed "like a young king. Sensitive, but like steel." With some misgivings about his self-assurance, which bordered on arrogance, he was cast in the part and gave a splendid performance in what most agree was the greatest antiwar picture ever made. Ayres had read the book and developed strong feelings not only about the role but also about the character's pacificist sentiments.

After that film Lew Ayres was one of Hollywood's most popular leading men. Some of his leading ladies were the late Constance Bennett in *Common Clay* (1930), the late Lillian Harvey in *My Weakness* (1933), Alice Faye in *She Learned About Sailors* (1934), Alice White (now a secretary in Hollywood) in *Cross Country Cruise* (1934), and Joan Perry (who later married Harry Cohn) in *Panic on the Air* (1936).

Two years after *Panic,* the famous *Dr. Kildare* series, which continued for four years and nine features, began. Although the films in the series were low-budget programmers, the features were among M-G-M's top money-makers.

With the subsequent outbreak of World War II, Ayres was among the first of the stars to be called into service. Few in Hollywood had as clean an image, but when induction time came, he put his convictions—and career —on the line and declared himself a conscientious objector. Most of the press damned him. Thousands of fans wrote to his studio telling how he had been their favorite star but that now he was a coward and a traitor. Many United States theatres refused to show his pictures.

Lew spent the war years as a medic's and chaplain's aide and was discharged as a sergeant with three battle stars for the Luzon, Hollandia (Kotabaru), and Leyte invasions.

On his return to Hollywood, Lew was not generally warmly received but with the war over, some of the press and fellow actors did extend themselves to welcome him. He got off to a good start with the resumption of his career with parts in two hits of the era, *The Dark Mirror* (1946) and *Johnny Belinda* (1948). But Ayres was getting a little old for his former image, and his agent did not come up with any character work.

In 1956, he got excellent reviews for a documentary he put together called *Altars of the East,* a religious film, which appeared later in book form. In 1957, Secretary of State Dulles appointed him to a three-year term on the United States National Committee for UNESCO, and the following year Lew was hosting *Frontier Justice* on television.

Of the six Ayres films between *Johnny Belinda* and *The Carpetbaggers* (1964), only *Advise and Consent* (1962) was a quality product. Occasionally he can be seen on television shows such as *Hawaii Five-O* and *Here Come the Brides.*

His first wife was Lola Lane, from 1930 to 1933, when she divorced him on cruelty charges. In 1934 Mary Brian and Janet Gaynor ** were the bridesmaids when he married Ginger Rogers. They were divorced in 1936. In 1964 Lew married his present wife, former stewardess Diana Hall. None of his marriages has produced children.

The Ayres live in a bungalow in the Brentwood section of Los Angeles. He sees very few people connected with the movie industry, but occasionally visits Carl Laemmle, Jr., who first showed faith in him. Lew is very interested in peace, social justice, and astronomy, in that order. He answers yes to whether he would again declare himself against the Vietnam war. He regularly refuses to participate in programs or interviews about his early pictures, stating, "There are so many important things to be thinking and talking about. I really don't see how people can waste precious time on such irrelevancies."

At home in Brentwood. *Jon Virzi*

As she looked in pictures during the late thirties.

SPRING BYINGTON

America's favorite screen mother-in-law was born in Colorado Springs, Colorado, in 1893. Her father, a college professor, died when she was five years old. Her mother was a doctor. She encouraged the child to choose a profession, and at age fourteen Spring announced she was going to be an actress. While in high school, Spring and a fellow student began an acting company on five hundred dollars she had inherited. They toured mining camps in the area. When she finished school she visited a casting office in Kansas City and applied for a job with the Stewart Walker Stock Company, which was leaving for a tour of Canada. It was a professional company but Spring was confident she would get a part. "That's the wonderful thing about innocence, or ignorance; you aren't a bit frightened because you just don't know enough to be," she says about her early years. She traveled with them for a number of years. She had a few lean seasons and was stranded now and then, but once she embarked on an acting career there was no turning back. Also, she was completely on her own now that her mother had died.

With the coming of World War I, she left for Buenos Aires to join a repertory company, married the manager, Roy Chandler, and remained in South America for five years, leaving when she and her husband separated. They had two daughters, Phyllis and Lois. It was Spring's only marriage.

After returning to the States she made her Broadway debut in *A Beggar on Horseback* (1924). After that she did other plays, *The Great Adventure* (1926), *To-night at Twelve* (1928), and *Be Your Age* (1929). In *Age* she achieved her life-long ambition: to see her name in lights on a Broadway marquee. Unfortunately, the play closed after three performances.

In the spring of 1933, RKO was casting its prestige picture of the year, the Louisa May Alcott classic, *Little Women*. The casting director's candidate for the part of Mrs. March was not the producer's. Stewart Walker, then with the studio, suggested they compromise with Spring Byington, who had never made a film. Her Marmee in the film proved to be as warm and human as all the other characters she would play in dozens of movies thereafter. During the thirties for Twentieth Century-Fox she played Mother Jones in a series of seventeen Jones Family feature films, she was in *Mutiny on the Bounty* (1935), *Dodsworth* (1936), *Penrod and Sam* (1937) with Billy and Bobby Mauch (both are film editors and live in Los Angeles), *Jezebel* (1938), *You Can't Take It with You* (1938), her favorite, *The Story of Alexander Graham Bell* (1939), *Meet John Doe* (1941), *Roxie Hart* (1942), and *The Enchanted Cottage* (1945).

Undoubtedly, Spring Byington is best remembered for the television series *December Bride,* which began as a radio program. The television version went on the air over CBS October 4, 1954, and ran five full seasons. It was written by Park Levey who patterned Spring's character after his own mother-in-law. Frances Rafferty, who played Spring's daughter, was the sister of Max Rafferty, the right-wing California politician. She and Spring became quite close and remained so until Frances's death.

Since *December Bride* went off the air, Spring has made a few guest appearances on such programs as *Batman* and *I Dream of Jeannie.* On a recent visit to relatives in South America, she was recognized wherever she went, thanks to reruns of her television show. Spring still gets offers for running parts on television but she has no desire to work hard or be tied down for long. "I'm doing exactly as I please these days and it's very agreeable," she says. She lives alone in a small house in the Hollywood hills.

She has always gotten on well with her sons-in-law, but when her daughters were growing up they complained at times that their mother belonged more to her own career than to them. Spring is one of those performers who loses her true identity to the character she plays. She plans someday to visit Europe, something she never had time for. She spends considerable time reading science fiction and is keenly interested in metaphysics.

At home in the Hollywood hills. *Alice May*

In her prom dress from the highly successful 1945 film *Junior Miss*.

PEGGY ANN GARNER

The child star of the 1940s was born in Canton, Ohio, in 1931. Her parents separated when she was four years old and her mother took Peggy Ann to New York City where she did very well modeling children's clothes for John Robert Powers. Two years later they went to Hollywood where, thanks to her aggressive mother, she appeared in *Little Miss Thoroughbred* (1938). Peggy Ann then won the role of Carole Lombard's daughter in *In Name Only* (1939). She reverted to small roles in such films as *Blondie Brings Up Baby* (1939), *Abe Lincoln in Illinois* (1940), *Eagle Squadron* (1942), and *Jane Eyre* (1944).

Peggy Ann had been placed under contract to Twentieth Century-Fox in 1943. After making *Jane Eyre*, her mother had learned that M-G-M had offered to buy half of her Fox contract and wanted to cast her in the role of the boyish girl in a large budget picture they planned called *National Velvet*. She learned also that Darryl F. Zanuck had refused the offer. When she asked for an explanation she was told that Fox was buying another property with an even better role for her daughter. The part in *National Velvet* (1945) went to Elizabeth Taylor, with whom Peggy Ann had worked in *Jane Eyre*. The book Zanuch referred to was purchased, Miss Garner was cast in a key role, and a new director named Elia Kazan was hired. The result of it all was that the film *A Tree Grows in Brooklyn* turned out to be one of the best pictures of that era, and Fox made a fortune and had a new star, Peggy Ann Garner. Not only did the public make the film one of the biggest box-office successes of the year but when Academy Award time came around, Peggy Ann was awarded a miniature statuette of the coveted Oscar for "the outstanding child actress of 1945."

Peggy Ann made a few good films after that, but only a few. Her fan mail, mostly from teen-age girls who identified with the somewhat plain actress, was enormous, and the fan magazines hung on her every move. She appeared in *Keys of the Kingdom* (1944), *Junior Miss* (1945), from the hit Broadway play, *Home, Sweet Homicide* (1946), and *Daisy Kenyon* (1947). After that it was downhill all the way, although the performances she turned in were always good. She played opposite Johnny Sheffield ** in a Monogram cheapie, *Bomba, the Jungle Boy* (1949), then did *Teresa* (1951), and *Black Widow* (1954). Her next film was *The Cat* (1966).

From 1950 to 1960 Peggy Ann lived, worked, and studied in New York City, where she says she "learned her craft." She stayed much of the time with Ed Sullivan, whose daughter is a close friend, and studied for a short time with the Actors Studio until they began to undermine her confidence in her acting ability. In 1950 she debuted in New York with Dorothy Gish in *The Man*. Then there was *A Royal Family* in 1951 and *Home Is the Hero* three years later. It was also during that period that she worked constantly on live television in New York and in summer stock.

Peggy Ann has had three marriages, all ending in divorce. Albert Salmi was her second. The year after that ended, in 1963, she married a real estate broker. She now lives with her daughter by Salmi, fourteen-year-old Cass— who also wants to act—in a small apartment in Brentwood, California.

She speaks without bitterness about losing the starring role in the smash play *Bus Stop* to Kim Stanley in 1955. She was the first choice of the playwright William Inge. She did the road company but the credit was not enough to reactivate her career, as the Broadway production would have done. Of Miss Stanley's performance, she says: "I never believed her for one minute." Of her teen-age years as a movie star, Peggy Ann would not trade them for any "normal" childhood. She insists that her mother always provided time for dates, sports, and studies.

Her only friends from her star period are Jane Withers and Lon McCallister, who gave Peggy Ann her first screen kiss.

Although she has an agent and still considers herself in the running for suitable roles, Peggy Ann holds down a full-time job as sales manager in charge of fleet sales for a Pontiac dealer in Santa Monica, California.

Informally at home in her apartment.
Gary Leavitt

The pride of the Tigers, 1940. *UPI*

CHARLES GEHRINGER

The greatest second baseman in American League history was born in 1904 on a farm near Fowlerville, Michigan. His German-born parents were unable to understand why their son neglected his duties around their property to play ball instead. Charles's father died before the boy made a name for himself but his mother admitted in an interview years after Charles had become nationally famous that she had scolded herself many times over the years for thinking of her farm rather than her son's abilities and inclinations. Gehringer and his mother lived together until she died in 1946.

A scout for the Detroit Tigers spotted Charlie during an amateur game and signed him up in 1924. He had never played second base before. Many felt that Ty Cobb, who ran the ball club, had no confidence in Gehringer, but Cobb and Charlie have denied it several times. In fact, Charlie credits Cobb with giving him several valuable pointers.

For several seasons Charlie played with the independent team in Angola, Indiana, but in 1927 the Tigers felt he was ready to play big-time baseball. During the next thirteen seasons Gehringer's batting fell below .300 only once, in 1932, when he slipped to .298.

Gehringer played in the World Series of 1934, 1935, and 1940. He was also chosen for six All Star games. In 1937 he was picked the Most Valuable Player in the American League.

When the Tigers played the Cardinals in the 1934 series Charlie batted .379 for seven games. His eleven hits included a home run off Dizzy Dean **and his brother Paul. The next year against the Cubs he batted .375 in six games and established a record for second baseman by handling thirty-five chances safely. By the time he retired in 1942 to enter the service he had played twenty-three hundred games. He did not return to play but managed the Tigers for two years beginning in 1951. The last time he played anywhere was in 1965 at the Old Timers Game at Yankee Stadium.

In 1938 Gehringer had formed a partnership with Ray Forsyth, whom he met several years before when Ray sold him a Hupmobile. They started a company to manufacture a new kind of upholstery button, and within a few years most of the big auto manufacturers were their customers. The firm, Gehringer and Forsyth, now turn out automotive interior trim, such as seating fabrics, leather, vinyls, and carpeting, as well as a separate line of alloys for furnaces. Charlie's salary as vice-president is over twice what he would be getting as the Tigers' top player.

His association with the ball club ended completely in 1959, when he was not reelected to the board of directors. He has, however, remained an avid fan and seldom misses a home game—if it is played at night. When baseball is not in season he can be found "trying to root the Lions football team and the Red Wings hockey team in." His wife, whom he married in 1949, the year he was elected to the Baseball Hall of Fame, says she sees very little of him during weekend daylight hours. "Charlie believes in really keeping fit," she said. "If he isn't watching a sport, he's playing one. His current favorite is golf. I keep telling him that the way he keeps himself in trim I'm going to look like his mother. He looks the same as the day I married him." The couple have no children. They live on five acres of land in Birmingham, Michigan, ten miles from Charlie's Detroit office.

In 1969 the Baseball Writers Association voted him the Greatest Living Second Baseman.

The Greatest Living Second Baseman today. *Clifford May*

With Paramount, 1938.

SYLVIA SIDNEY

The screen heroine of the depression era was born Sophia Kosow in 1910 to Russian immigrant parents in the Bronx. When she was eleven years old she decided to act, and four years later left high school and joined the Theatre Guild School. But she was soon dismissed for refusing to abide by the rules, such as being in by a certain hour at night. She became obsessed with the idea of showing them up and threw herself into a frenzy of auditions.

Hounding the offices of agents and casting directors, Sylvia got parts in touring companies that took her to Colorado and Washington. She made her Broadway debut in the 1926 production of *The Squall*. Two years later she created something of a sensation with her piercing scream in *The Gods of the Lightning*. Fox studios brought her to Hollywood to give the same chilling shriek in *Thru Different Eyes* (1929) .

Sylvia had a waiflike quality that evoked immediate sympathy and projected great intensity. In an era full of strikes, poverty, and social reform, she was the perfect actress to portray a working girl in trouble. And trouble was something her pictures had plenty of. She was pregnant and unmarried in *An American Tragedy* (1931) , trapped in tenement life in the classic *Street Scene* (1931) , in jail in *Ladies of the Big House* (1932) , wanted by the police in *Mary Burns—Fugitive* (1935) , the girl friend of a wanted man in *Fury* (1936) , and the sister of a criminal living in the slums in *Dead End* (1937) . Some of her other efforts are *Trail of the Lonesome Pine* (1936) , *The Wagons Roll at Night* (1941) , *Blood on the Sun* (1945) , *Les Miserables* (1952) , and *Behind the High Wall* (1956) , her last film.

The personal life of the petite actress has been nearly as troubled as her screen roles. She was married for several months in 1935 to publisher Bennett Cerf. Her union with Luther Adler began in 1938 and lasted nine years. They have one son, Jody. Her three-year marriage to Carlton Alsop ended in divorce in 1950. During most of her years at Paramount studios movie people gossiped about her affair with production chief B. P. Schulberg, father of the writer Budd Schulberg.

Sylvia did a lot of television during the fifties. One of her most outstanding parts during that period was the star's mother in television's *The Helen Morgan Story* in 1957. By this time she had made a complete and very successful transition into character work.

After entering films Sylvia had returned to the stage several times in such vehicles as *Bad Girl*, in which she played an unwed mother in 1930, *The Gentle People* (1939) with the late Franchot Tone, and *A Very Special Baby* (1956) with her former husband Luther Adler.

Her last Broadway performance was as Alan Arkin's mother in *Enter Laughing* in 1963. Since then she has toured in several road companies. In one, which had no other name actors, she was billed fourth. When she makes television and radio appearances to plug her plays she usually takes along a copy of her book on needlepoint that has been in print for several years and is considered among the best in its category.

Several years ago Miss Sydney gave up her Manhattan apartment and moved to a house in Washington, Connecticut, where she lives with her two Pekingese. Aside from advancing years, one of the former star's main problems seems to be her disposition. As far back as forty years ago she fought with the late Josef von Sternberg when he directed her. One of those associated with the production of *Auntie Mame*, in which she starred at the New York City Center in 1958, said recently, "We wanted her for the role because so many of us had liked her work over the years, but she was nothing but trouble from the day we signed the contract."

Now active as a character actress.

In 1939, already gray. *NBC Radio*

JOHN F. KIERAN

The intellectual from the golden age of radio was born in New York City in 1892 to parents he has called "poor but Irish." His father, Mike, was a scholar who taught classics at Hunter College. His mother, Kate Donahue, wrote poetry and taught in the public schools, and had numerous children of her own. When John Francis Kieran was ten, the family were fully aware of his unusual intelligence even among children far above average. His first intense interest seemed to be music but then he branched out quickly to languages, sports, ornithology, and literature. He made the high school varsity basketball team, was considered an expert swimmer and diver, and won a newspaper golf championship.

Then came Fordham University, where he graduated cum laude in 1912, and a teaching job in a country school in Dutchess County, New York. He had six pupils, which brought him ten dollars a week, and he ran a poultry business on the side. In the fall of 1913 John became timekeeper for a sewer-construction project. Most of the workers were Italian and in a short time he was fluent in the language, after which he mastered French. His career as a journalist began in 1915 when he joined the *New York Times* sports department. During World War I John was with the Eleventh Engineers and spent two years in Europe. He returned to the United States, was mustered out, and hired by the old *Herald Tribune,* which lost him after a time to the Hearst syndicate. He joined the *Times* in 1927 to pen that paper's first daily by-line column. John resigned from the *Times* sports department in 1943 and spent a year on the now defunct *New York Sun.*

Kieran's fame dates to when he joined a panel of experts on radio's *Information Please* in 1938. His weekly salary as a panelist was five hundred dollars. During his twelve-year stint on the weekly coast-to-coast program he displayed a knowledge of subjects so diverse that often he was referred to as the man who knows everything. Listeners often addressed their letters containing questions meant to stump him to "Mr. Know-It-All." Not only was he familiar with totally unrelated matters, he went beyond reciting facts and figures: his replies to questions usually showed a deep understanding of the considered field. In 1948 Kieran was also being featured in an NBC television series, *John Kieran's Kaleidoscope*. Three years later the network brought him back to do *Treasures of New York*. All the while he kept writing. Among his books are *The Story of the Olympic Games* (1936), *Nature Notes* (1941), *American Sporting Scene* (1943), *Footnotes on Nature* (1947), and *Natural History of New York City* (1959). In 1969 when *Books I Love*, his last, was published, his works had sold over three hundred fifty thousand copies.

He earned a footnote in history books when he coined the term "Brain Trust," referring to the small group of technicians and scholars who helped formulate Franklin D. Roosevelt's 1932 campaign for the presidency. Kieran at the time was the *Time*'s man in Albany reporting on FDR, who was then governor of New York.

He and his wife Margaret Ford, whom he married in 1947 after he became a widower, reside in Rockport, Massachusetts, in a house they call "The Headlands." His children by his first wife, Alma Boldtmann, are James and John, Jr., both Yale graduates, and Beatrice. Still an avid reader forever widening his interests and knowledge, he devotes late afternoons and evenings to reading. Each morning he rises before dawn and walks in the woods that surround his house or along the New England shore familiarizing himself with the birds and insects.

His former fellow panelist Clifton Fadiman, asked about him recently, replied that Kieran was "the sweetest, most gentle man I've encountered. The only man I know who was not terribly impressed by John's intelligence was John."

A bit grayer today. *Erich Hartmann*

Arriving in the United States, 1931. *UPI*

ALEXANDRA TOLSTOY

The twelfth (and only living) of Leo Tolstoy's thirteen children, was born on the famed writer's estate, Yasnaya Polyana, in 1884, the youngest girl in the family. While not her father's favorite, she was probably the closest to him. In 1901 she became his secretary and when he died of pneumonia in 1910 she was preparing him to escape from his wife and remaining children, who opposed his views. As executrix of his estate, Alexandra bought back Yasnaya Polyana from the peasants to whom he had willed it, and installed a racing stable. She then toured Europe for four years, until World War I began. During the holocaust, she was gassed on the Armenian front and received several decorations.

When Russia left the war and the Soviets took the reins of government from Alexander Kerensky,* Alexandra, with official approval, founded the Society for the Dissemination of Tolstoy's Works. She says she always opposed the Soviet government and never had any faith in its integrity but she did seek work under Soviet approval in several undertakings, and being the daughter of the country's greatest writer alone saved her from the firing squad. Nevertheless, she was arrested five times for allowing White Russians to hold clandestine meetings in her house, and spent several years in prison for her activities. Her almost cheerful adaptation to prison diet and conditions surprised fellow inmates and jailers alike.

Like her father, Alexandra values work as very good for the soul, practically an end in itself. She still cannot watch anyone working without feeling a strong sense of guilt for being born a countess, a title she was forbidden to use after the revolution.

In 1929 Alexandra secured permission to journey to Japan for a lecture tour, and never returned to Russia. Two years later she came to the United States on the same pretense, and remains. With large contributions from White Russian emigrés and right-wing organizations, she founded the Tolstoy Foundation, which now has farms and buildings throughout the Western world. The foundation provides a home for aging Russians and a start for those who have left Russia to begin anew. She herself lives in Valley Cottage, on Reed Farm, the fifty-acre foundation farm in New York.

Although her father was anticlerical, there is a Russian Orthodox Church at the farm and she is a member of the congregation.

Her manner of dress, which has been likened to an unmade bed, is as eccentric as her ideas and living habits. Now in her eighties, she writes and edits every day for several hours and then turns to hard manual labor. She lives in a tiny room and has even given up her one relative luxury, smoking. Her only diversion is fishing, which she does after rising at 4:30 A.M.

She has never married or even considered a man seriously as her life is devoted to spreading her father's ideas and fighting communism. Anyone familiar with Leo Tolstoy's beliefs, however, would look in vain for much similarity in Alexandra Lvovna Tolstoy's preachments. She is in constant demand by conservative women's clubs to tell them all the things they want most to hear, though her greatest condemnation of communism is that it robs the people of their freedom. Her remedy for the social unrest in America: "There is too much freedom here. We need less. There would be fewer riots." When confronted with a question she cannot answer she replies in terms so vague that even her sponsors are somewhat embarrassed. When asked about Czechoslovakia's uprising she replied, "The will of the people should prevail." When challenged on the basis of her not having set foot in Russia in over forty years, she says that nothing has changed. The world figure she admires most and considers the leading expert on Russia is Richard M. Nixon, whom she thinks her father—whose ideas helped fashion the background of the Russian Revolution—would approve of.

At the Tolstoy farm recently. *Diana Keyt*

Among the top male box-office draws, 1943.

RANDOLPH SCOTT

The "strong, silent-type" actor was born on his father's country place in Orange County, Virginia, in 1903. His grandfather at fourteen fought with Stonewall Jackson. During World War I Randolph, or Randy, at thirteen, already six feet tall, lied about his age to join the army and fought in France. After the war he attended Georgia Tech, and until he hurt his knee, played on the football team. After that he took a degree from the University of North Carolina and then met and became friends with Howard Hughes on a golf course. Cecil B. De Mille—who saw him at the Cocoanut Grove, and was interested in him for a part—suggested he get some training. So instead of returning home to work as an engineer for his dad, Scott cashed in his return train ticket and enrolled at the Pasadena Playhouse. He had to sleep on a bed far too short for his six-foot three-inch frame, so Hughes bought him an extra long one.

He started in movies in *Women Men Marry* (1931) opposite Loretta Young's sister, Sally Blaine. Between picture parts he acted in such plays as *Under a Virginia Moon* and *Broken Wing* in Los Angeles theatres. Then he started to work steadily, though in small roles, in such films as *Broken Dreams* (1933) with Martha Sleeper (the proprietress of a dress shop in San Juan, Puerto Rico), and *To the Last Man* (1933) with Esther Ralston.** He was Helen Gahagan Douglas's * leading man in the 1935 version of *She* and played with Heather Angel (retired, married, and living in Santa Barbara, California) in *The Last of the Mohicans* (1936). After Mae West chose him for *Go West, Young Man* (1936) his career really began to gain momentum. He was in *High, Wide and Handsome* (1937) with Irene

Dunne,* *Road to Reno* (1938) with Hope Hampton (a Manhattan resident), and *Jesse James* (1939). Cary Grant, with whom he shared a beach house for some time, costarred with Randy and Irene Dunne in *My Favorite Wife* (1940), and in 1941 Randy was leading man to Elisabeth Bergner * in *Paris Calling. The Spoilers* (1942) and *Pittsburgh* (1942) followed.

From then on, Randolph Scott made practically nothing but war films and Westerns, even his best not being among the period's finest films. But until *Ride the High Country* (1962), he remained among the top male box-office draws. Even then, it is doubtful that he would have retired had his health not been failing. He still receives staggering offers to act in a television series.

Scott, whose private life was never featured much in his publicity, lives in Beverly Hills, just off Sunset Boulevard with his third wife, Pat Sillman, nineteen years his junior, who gave him a child, Christopher. They were married in 1944 after he divorced Marion Somerville, a childhood sweetheart who also happened to be a member of the Du Pont family. During their marriage, which began in 1936, her horse Battleship won the Grand National, the British steeplechase. That was in 1938.

Because his former home in Los Angeles had adjoined the golf course of the Los Angeles Country Club, Randy was offered, and accepted, a membership, only to find that he was the only actor ever to be admitted to that very snobbish club. He resigned, but rejoined after his retirement. Randy visits his office in Beverly Hills almost daily to oversee his business interests. He and his wife are seldom seen at premieres or parties, and Randy refuses to grant interviews, giving the excuse that he is now completely retired. Another reason is that he suffers from poor hearing.

At a recent Hollywood opening. *Jon Virzi*

Spanky gives advice to one of Our Gang, 1935.

SPANKY McFARLAND

The fat boy of *Our Gang* comedies was born in Fort Worth, Texas, in 1928. When "Spanky" (George Emmett McFarland) was two years old his aunt sent his photograph to producer Hal Roach in Hollywood. Roach had always used a fat boy among the regular kids in the gang. (The original was "Fat Joe" Cobb, now living on Clarington Avenue in Los Angeles.)

Spanky was placed under contract and his family moved to Hollywood. He stayed with the series until it expired under M-G-M auspices in 1944. He was sixteen at the time and had made over one hundred fifty features and shorts. Aside from the *Our Gang* two-reelers, he appeared in *Kidnapped* (1938) with Freddie Bartholomew,* *Trail of the Lonesome Pine* (1936) with Henry Fonda, and *Johnny Doughboy* (1942) with Jane Withers (now widowed and living in Encino, California) .

For a time Spanky tried being a free-lance actor but with no luck. Because he had never considered doing anything else, life in any other business was difficult, and dull. He served a stretch in the United States Army and then tried selling insurance and found that his acting helped him develop a faculty for dealing with people. He then sold automobiles and wholesaled Coca-Cola, and briefly he ran his own restaurant until legal complications developed: his landlord disappeared and his lease was cancelled. His next job was at an aircraft plant, which he didn't like, and his first marriage had ended in divorce.

In the late 1950s Spanky began free-lancing in television, usually doing commercials. However it got him a regular job in Tulsa, Oklahoma, where he hosted a children's daily television show. It gave him an opportunity to alter the approach he had always despised: kiddie entertainers who dress and try to act like children. "Kid shows are always playing down," he said. "It's silly to have a grown man sitting there trying to be a kid. Kids know better." Among the old movies he introduced on each day's show were many he made with Alfalfa (shot to death in a quarrel in January 1959), Buckwheat Thomas (killed in 1968 flying food to Biafra), and Darla Hood.** Spanky is in touch only with Darla, who writes to him from time to time. One of the regulars, child actor Robert Blake, played a murderer in *In Cold Blood* (1968).

Following his television stint, Spanky became sales manager for an Oklahoma wine company and realized that what he liked best was selling. It was the one executive job open to him with his limited education. (His high school diploma was earned while serving in the army.)

In 1966, Spanky, his wife, and their thirteen-year-old son and eight-year-old daughter moved to Cinnaminson, New Jersey, near Philadelphia. He became a sales-training supervisor for the Philco-Ford Company, teaching salesmen in the Philadelphia area how to sell television sets. They call him George, as at home, but not because he has any regrets about his childhood. He admits having been paid very well for his movie work, and enjoying it. If his career left any deep scars, he does not seem to be aware of them. "I had a ball," he says, and recalls that he was eight or nine before he realized that most children did not act in movies.

George occasionally watches one of his old shorts on television, but with a critical eye, wincing at some of the bits he feels he overacted. However, he would love to get back into television as a pitchman on commercials, and has no objection to his children going into show business, but he will not encourage them. If and when they ask his permission, all he intends telling them is, "You're on your own, sweetie."

A business executive now.

By 1941, one of the top female vocalists in the country. *NBC*

GINNY SIMS

The popular female vocalist of the 1940s was born in San Antonio, Texas, on May 25, 1916. Her real name is Virginia Sims. Her father, the manager of the local movie theatre, moved the family to California when Ginny was very young.

Ginny's original intention was to become a teacher. With that in mind she enrolled in the Fresno State Teachers College. College dance bands were the craze at the time, and Ginny soon organized a college trio, which was to sing with the local and visiting groups, but people kept telling her that she ought to try to make it as a single.

At eighteen she won an audition with Guy Lombardo. Even though she didn't get the job, she was greatly encouraged by the comments her numbers drew from professionals. She began singing with small bands and then landed a spot with Tommy Gerun's group, a band fairly well known during the 1930s. The male vocalist with Gerun at that time was Al Norris, later to become famous as Tony Martin.

Ginny's big break came when she went with Kay Kyser in the late 1930s. Kyser in those days had one of the hottest orchestras in the business. Not only was his musical sound very popular but he was a big name on radio with his *Kollege of Musical Knowledge,* a quiz program with music. Ginny worked in skits as well as songs with the male vocalist Harry Babbitt (now a salesman at Leisure World, the South Laguna Beach senior-citizen project) and the show's comic, Ishkabibble (living in Australia under his real name, Merwyn A. Bogue).

The Kyser-Sims liaison was more than professional and for a time Ginny wanted very much to marry the band leader. But as her interest waned, his increased, and near the end it was Kyser who was insisting that they make it legal. They parted completely but amicably in September 1941 when Ginny signed for a radio series sponsored by Kleenex tissues. Ginny continued as a performer right into the fifties, but her few years with Kyser were the high points of her career.

In 1945 she married engineer Hyatt Dehn and had two children by him, David and Conrad, before they were divorced in March 1951. Two months later she married Bob Calhoun, an oilman. They separated the following September and were divorced in October.

Ginny made several films with Kay Kyser and a number of others on her own including *That's Right—You're Wrong* (1939), *You'll Find Out* (1940), *Playmates* (1941), *Here We Go Again* (1942) with Edgar Bergen,** *Hit the Ice* (1943), *Broadway Rhythm* (1944), and *Shady Lady* (1945).

In 1958 she returned to the Maisonette of the Hotel St. Regis in New York where she had last played a decade before. There were other engagements but they failed to reactivate her career.

In 1962 Ginny married Don Eastvold, who had become her partner in a real estate development in the Salton Sea area of the California desert. For a while one of their salesmen was Ishkabibble. The project did not work out financially, although the Eastvolds managed to build and run a club there for a while. They then moved to a similar undeveloped area in Minnesota that turned out to be a disaster for all involved, and the Eastvolds are being sued by a number of parties who hold very hard feelings about the outcome.

Ginny and her husband moved from Minnesota to Chevy Chase, Maryland, and then to Hollywood, their last known address. In 1969 the legal difficulties concerning the Minnesota fiasco became so great that the couple disappeared completely. George Dunning, who once arranged for Kay Kyser, and is a long-time friend of Ginny's, refuses to tell anyone where she is but hints that she and her husband have left the country to avoid lawsuits and possible prosecution.

Her last performance. *Al Woodbury*

When he was broadcasting from Chicago's Palmer House Hotel, 1935.

SHEP FIELDS

The band leader who became famous for his "rippling rhythm" sound was born in Brooklyn in 1911. After graduating from Erasmus High School he attended Saint John's University for a year. In 1929 after his father, Jack, a newspaperman, died, Shep got a job playing saxophone in a dance band to earn a living. By 1934 he was playing the Hotel Pierre in New York with his own band, earning a living, but without a reputation or recognition. Then Jules Stein, head of the MCA talent agency, dropped in with the famous dance team Veloz and Yolanda (no longer working; they live apart in Los Angeles), looking for a band to travel with them around the country. Shep signed on. (He thought that they really wanted Freddy Martin's organization but that Martin refused the job.) The billing read "Veloz and Yolanda Orchestra under the direction of Shep Fields." They played the Palmer House in Chicago and were heard over the Mutual Network.

Fields was unhappy playing second fiddle to the dancing couple and also because his band lacked a distinctive style. With the best of his musicians he copied segments of other musical manners that were popular with top bands such as Wayne King's and Eddy Duchin's. Shep was happy enough with his new sound. When Veloz and Yolanda parted for an engagement at the Cocoanut Grove in Los Angeles, he called the owner of the Pierre and got back his old job, with more money. On the way, the band stopped off in Rockford, Illinois, to play a one-nighter. Later, Shep and his wife Evy were sipping a soda in a local drugstore when she blew into her straw, making a gurgling sound. Shep admits that it sounds like a scene from a Ruby Keeler musical, but it actually inspired one of the most successful sounds of the decade. From that day on he opened every performance and broadcast standing before the microphone and blowing through a straw into a small bowl of water. He swears to this day that he even had to have special bowls because not every bowl would produce the exact sound he was after. The name rippling rhythm was the result of a contest, with four hundred winners out of five thousand replies. They all had the same winning suggestion. No one got the prize, a weekend at the Palmer House. The band made two films: *Rippling Rhythm* (1937) and *Big Broadcast of 1938,* both shown constantly around the country on television on the *Late Show.*

Though there was no evidence that the public had tired of it, in 1941 Shep decided to give up rippling rhythm and developed what pop-music critic John Simon has called "one of the most musical dance bands of all time." With Shep playing the reeds, the group continued with their new style until 1947 when they returned to the sound audiences still clamored for. They stuck with it until Fields disbanded the group in 1963.

His brother Freddie, who had started out as a trombone player, had by this time become one of the most powerful agents in Hollywood. Shep joined Freddie, who is married to singer Polly Bergen, as an executive with Creative Management Associates, which represents some of the top names in show business. Another brother, Elliot, is a vice-president. Shep is a troubleshooter, journeying between his Beverly Hills office and Las Vegas, where much of their business is placed.

Sometimes he will get a letter from a teen-ager who wants to know where he can buy his records. Shep, too, listens now and then to some of the old records made years ago when the band was grossing $1 million annually. The rippling rhythm still sounds pretty good to him. "We were lucky from the very beginning," he says.

An executive at Creative Management Associates, Beverly Hills. *Diana Keyt*

Helen (Julie Stevens) and Gil Whitney (David Gothard), 1948. *CBS Radio*

HELEN TRENT: Julie Stevens

". . . a woman who sets out to prove what so many women long to prove in their own lives, that romance can live on at thirty-five, and even beyond." Thus began 203 CBS affiliate radio stations five days a week broadcasting the trials and tribulations of Helen Trent, middle-aged Hollywood fashion designer. As many as four million listeners tuned in to the show that opened and closed to "Juanita," hummed by Stanley Davis accompanying himself on the guitar. Davis was also the producer-director, under the guidance of Frank and Anne Hummert.

Helen's men included a millionaire, gangster, movie star, hypnotist, and even a psychotic, but her fans knew that her real love was the handsome lawyer Gil Whitney, played by David Gothard (now residing in Los Angeles). Many times they nearly married, the postponements became one of radio's running gags. The series began with Virginia Clark in Chicago in 1933. Her husband had disappeared at sea, and she lived with her companion, an old maid, Agatha Anthony, played by Bess McCammon, now deceased.

Helen became so popular and so fixed was her image that when, following the script, she once ventured into the stateroom of a male fellow passenger while on a pleasure cruise, the network was flooded with mail demanding a proper explanation. Despite her established chic dress and manner, her creators had welded a fictional character of spotless reputation. She may have lived in Hollywood but her morals were above reproach.

Julie Stevens replaced the original Helen when the series moved to New York in 1944, the year she married Charles Underhill, a businessman, between programs. Auditions for the "New York" Helen had been held on a rainy day which coincided with the last broadcast of *Kitty Foyle,* a radio soap opera featuring Julie Stevens in the title role. Julie had walked across the street, and soaking wet and depressed, was greeted in the CBS lobby by an actress who had just finished auditioning for the role. "Julie," she said, "why on earth did you come over on a day like this for this part. Dear, you are far too young to play the role."

Nearly as famous as Helen, but never enjoying her popularity, was Cynthia Swanson, the millionairess widow who managed to marry Gil Whitney for a time. Her part was written and played for a heavy, and was acted by Mary Jane Higby, at the time the star of radio's *When a Girl Marries*. Mary Jane in her autobiography *Tune in Tomorrow* (1968) recounts her life as daytime radio's most hated character; most of her mail those days was unsigned and decidedly unflattering.

Unlike radio's *Ma Perkins* or *Just Plain Bill, Helen Trent* was not sought out by fans for advice. Instead she was inundated with suggestions for her love life. If she took her listeners' counsel to heart it must have been some of the worst advice ever given: she was constantly involved with suicides, murders, divorces, and assorted squabbles. According to Julie, Helen "was only sophisticated on the surface. Basically she was a very naïve girl."

Despite its continued high ratings, CBS decided to cancel the series. When the show closed with the broadcast of April 19, 1960, *Time* magazine ran an obituary giving it the title of the oldest of all soap operas, outlasting *Ma Perkins* by three weeks. The show had ended with Helen about to marry Gil, just short of the minister pronouncing them man and wife—in case it ever went back on the air. The Hummerts, the senior producers, were taking no chances.

Julie has appeared since in commercials for Chase Manhattan Bank, Hudson Paper Towels, and Bayer Aspirin. In 1968, with her husband and two teen-age girls, she moved from Armonk, New York, to Pittsburgh, where Mr. Underhill is district director of public relations for United States Steel. Since Helen was supposed to be at least thirty-five years old when she took on the role, she would now be over sixty.

Helen today. *Clifford May*

A Paramount publicity shot 1943.

CLIFF EDWARDS

Ukulele Ike was born in Hannibal, Missouri, to Edward, a railroad worker, and Nellie Edwards. As a little boy he sold newspapers and he still recalls seeing Mark Twain talking with townspeople on the front porch of the local hotel. Cliff left school at the age of fourteen to work for a short time in a shoe factory and then began singing illustrated songs. He traveled to Saint Louis where he sang for nickels in the saloons and played traps at the Palace Theatre. At one point he was chanting narration for silent movies, working fifteen shows a day for $3.50 a week.

Cliff began working a lot with a pianist named Bobby Carleton who wrote a song called "Ja Da" which the pair parleyed into one of the biggest hits of the twenties. Overnight Cliff became a big draw in the flourishing vaudeville circuits.

During one long run in a west-side Chicago café, a waiter named Spot, who could never remember Cliff's name, called him Ike. Since Cliff was accompanying himself on a ukulele, he took the name Ukulele Ike, his billing from then on, which became better known to the public than Cliff Edwards.

Before going out as a single, Cliff worked briefly with Lou Clayton, of Clayton, Jackson and Durante fame, and later with Peerce Keegan. He also played the drums and sang in an act with the late comedian Joe Frisco.

Cliff Edwards made it big in an era when anyone with a hit record was automatically a star. During the twenties and early thirties he had one hit after another. "June Night" sold 3.2 million records and "Sleepy Time Gal" went over a million. Many people today may associate "Toot, Toot, Tootsie Good-bye" with Al Jolson but it was Ukulele Ike who introduced and popularized it. Another of his hits was "I Cried for You," which sold 1.72 million records.

During this time in 1928 while playing the Orpheum Theatre in downtown Los Angeles he had a visit backstage from Irving Thalberg, then production head of M-G-M, who signed him to appear in *Hollywood Revue of 1929*. It was a part color talkie musical, in which Cliff introduced "Singing in the Rain." The picture, the song, and Cliff were all very well received. From then on, though he never received star billing, he worked constantly in films. In 1930 alone he appeared in seven features, among them *Dough Boys* with Sally Eilers and *Way Out West* with William Haines (now a successful Beverly Hills interior decorator).

Through the thirties and into the forties Edwards continued to make films and guest appearances on radio variety programs. He was practically a regular on Rudy Vallee's shows.

He developed a personal friendship with Walt Disney for whom he did the voice of Jiminy Cricket in the 1940 animated film *Pinocchio;* it was also Edwards who provided the voice for the film's hit song, "When You Wish Upon a Star."

From there began his real decline, which meant little or no work and the restrictions of a pensioner. The octogenarian's health has been poor these past years. He lives alone in a partly furnished apartment above Hollywood Boulevard. It is difficult for him to walk and he seldom leaves his house. Many years ago he was married briefly to a girl named Nancy Dover, but he has nothing to say about her other than that she was very pretty.

Disney Records a couple of years ago released an album on the Vista label entitled *Ukulele Ike Happens Again,* on which Cliff was backed by a jazz band while he sang some of his hit songs. But the voice that once sold over 74 million single records could not even sell out the first pressing.

Still playing twenty-seven years later.
Clifford May

In a scene from *I Was an Adventuress*, 1940.

VERA ZORINA

The ballerina-actress was born Eva Brigitta Hartwig on January 2, 1917, in Berlin where her Norwegian parents, Fritz and Billie, were living at the time.

Soon after she began to walk she was given a pair of ballet slippers, which she took to bed with her. Two years later she debuted as a butterfly in a flower ballet.

Her regular schooling was at the Lyceum for Girls in Berlin but she was trained for the dance by Olga Preobrajenska and Nicholas Legat. Legat had taught Pavlova and Nijinsky.

At the age of twelve she was presented to Max Reinhardt by dance impressario Anton Dolin. Reinhardt cast her in his *Midsummer Night's Dream* in 1929 and two years later in *The Tales of Hoffmann*.

Colonel de Basil and Leonide Massine saw her dancing at London's Gaiety Theatre in 1933 and induced her to join their Ballet Russe de Monte Carlo. De Basil and Massine explained that her name would have to be changed and presented her with a long list of Russian names from which to choose. She picked Vera Zorina for the simple reason it was the only one she could pronounce. However, since the troupe was made up predominantly of Russians, she felt obliged to study the language—nearly as religiously as her dancing. She danced with the company for three seasons, appearing at both Covent Garden in London and the Metropolitan Opera House in New York. It was during this period that she was linked romantically with André Eglevsky.

Vera then landed a lead role in the London company of *On Your Toes*. Movie producer Samuel Goldwyn saw her in the show and signed her to a contract, as much for her acting ability as for her dancing. In Hollywood, a big publicity campaign was undertaken. She made *The Goldwyn Follies* (1938), the year she married ballet director-choreographer George Balanchine, *On Your Toes* (1939), *I Was an Adventuress* (1940) with Richard Greene (living in London's Chelsea district), *Louisiana Purchase* (1941), *Star Spangled Rhythm* (1942) a year after becoming a United States citizen, and *Follow the Boys* (1944). She was the original choice for the role of Anna in *For Whom the Bell Tolls* (1943) but after two weeks of shooting Paramount took her off the picture and she was replaced by Ingrid Bergman. Whatever reason the producers had for the change, it was not revealed, but it was the kiss of death to her Hollywood career.

In 1938 Vera had made quite a success also on Broadway: she did *I Married an Angel;* she topped it two years later in *Louisiana Purchase,* which inspired one critic to call her "the hottest musical-comedy hit in a decade." Many hoped the beautiful new star would popularize ballet in films and Broadway musicals, but it never happened. In 1945 Margaret Webster presented her as Ariel in *The Tempest* and in 1947 she essayed the title role in *Joan of Arc at the Stake,* which was performed with the New York Philharmonic.

Her parting from Balanchine in 1946 was very expensive for him, and the following year she married Goddard Lieberson, president of Columbia Records. The parties in their East Sixties town house probably gather together more musical and dancing talent than could be found anywhere in the world for a social occasion. Along with having great influence in their fields they are also considered intellectuals and wits. They have two sons, Peter and Jonathan.

In recent years Vera, or Brigitta, as she is known to friends, has performed chiefly as a narrator. Her voice was heard on a number of record albums. The royalties went to charity. Also she narrated *Facade* with the Seattle Symphony. She has appeared in New York and throughout the country in narration of works by Hindemith, Stravinsky, and Honegger.

Vera has been active with the Lincoln Center as an adviser and director and for several seasons has been directing operas at the Santa Fe Opera Company in Santa Fe, New Mexico. She helped raise funds for a new $1.7 million theatre in the New Mexico hills.

At a recent opening. *UPI*

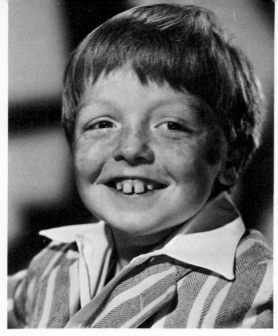

The sloe-eyed child star in 1947.

JACKIE "BUTCH" JENKINS

The child star of the 1940s was born in Los Angeles in 1937. His father was Captain Jack Jenkins of the United States Ferry Command. His mother was Doris Dudley, who had appeared on Broadway in such plays as *Moon and Sixpence* and *Here Come the Clowns* and a few Hollywood movies. Her father was Bide Dudley, a New York drama critic.

By the time he was six years old, Jackie had already earned a reputation among the lifeguards in Santa Monica as "the holy terror." In spite of all the trouble he got into, he was never thought of as a brat. However, his antics and high spirits were unusual for children then; most parents and educators were more interested in instilling discipline than in allowing free expression. Jackie once started a fire at home, but his mother wisely decided to keep a closer watch on her energetic little boy rather than curb his drives.

M-G-M was looking for just such a boy for the role of Ulysses Macauley in the film version of the William Saroyan novel *The Human Comedy* (1943). A Metro scout saw him one day on the beach and watched how he upset and charmed everyone who came in contact with him. Producer-director Clarence Brown (retired and living in Palm Springs, California) tested Jackie and then cast him in the picture along with Mickey Rooney and James Craig (living in Los Angeles). Butch, as most fans called him, had a total lack of theatrical mannerisms outstanding in most child actors at the time. He was certainly not good looking in the acceptable meaning of the phrase but his personality was overwhelming. He was something quite different in motion pictures. He was a real child.

Notwithstanding his making only nine movies in five years, Butch is very well remembered. Part of this is attributable to several of his other films

being on a par with *The Human Comedy*. He appeared with Ann Revere *
in *National Velvet* (1944) and Margaret O'Brien ** in *Our Vines Have
Tender Grapes* (1945). His others were *Boys' Ranch* (1946), *Little Mr. Jim*
(1946), *My Brother Talks to Horses* (1946), *The Big City* (1948) with
Betty Garrett (married to Larry Parks and living in Los Angeles's Nichols
Canyon), *The Bride Goes Wild* (1948), and *Summer Holiday* (1948), the
film musical version of Eugene O'Neill's *Ah, Wilderness*.

In 1947 Jackie's mother decided against her son continuing as an actor
and took him and his brother Ted to Dallas, Texas. She had been concerned
for some time about the pressure the studio had placed on the family and
worried about his inadequate schooling. When Jackie began to stutter she
felt she had no alternative.

After going through the lower schools and attending the State University
of Iowa, Jackie married in 1957. His wife gave him three daughters before
they were divorced in 1964. In 1966 he remarried. The Jenkinses live on
Lake Tawakoni in Quinlan, Texas, not far from Mother Jenkins who is the
developer of the exclusive Cloisters subdivision in Dallas. Butch is the owner
of several car washes and the East Texas Waters Systems which supplies
water to four Texas counties.

The six-foot-four-inch two-hundred-pound former star said recently,
"I have never regretted leaving the picture business and am very grateful to
my mother for taking me away from it. I enjoyed the first few years of acting
in movies but I certainly don't miss it. In fact, when I've had offers to return a few times I wasn't even tempted. There may be a better way to live
than on a lake with a couple of cows, a wife, and children but being a
movie star is not one."

The stutter that triggered his exit from Hollywood never left him.

As he looks today.

Under contract to Hal Wallis,
1950.

LIZABETH SCOTT

The deep-voiced movie star of the 1940s and 1950s was born Emma Matzo
in 1922 to an English father and Russian mother in Scranton, Pennsylvania.
She grew up there, graduating from Central High School and going to
Marywood College. After a summer of acting with the Mary Desmond Stock
Company in Lake Ariel, she was encouraged to continue in the profession.
She went to New York City where she made the rounds of casting offices in
between her acting lessons, all the while living in a three-dollar-a-week room.

In 1940 Lizabeth put in a grueling season on the road with *Hellzapoppin,*
sixty-four of her performances being for one-night stands, and for a while
she was with the Fifty-second Street Stock Company, playing Sadie Thompson in *Rain.*

Things began to happen for Lizabeth Scott when she landed an under-
study spot to Tallulah Bankhead, then in the original cast of the modern
classic *The Skin of Our Teeth* (1942). For seven months Liz sat backstage
ready to go on. Finally, she left. A month later Miss Bankhead was ill and
the producers put in a desperate call to Lizabeth. Her performance, as a
maid, got her a contract to Hal Wallis, who brought her to Hollywood.

A screen test of several years before had come to nothing, but this time
Lizabeth tested and won a part opposite Robert Cummings in *You Came
Along* (1945). Paramount's still department took two thousand photos of
her immediately after the picture's completion. Wallis and the studio had
high hopes but on balance Lizabeth got better treatment from the fans
than from Hollywood. Although they gave her such leading men as Hum-

phrey Bogart, Dick Powell, Charlton Heston, and Alan Ladd, none of the twenty-two features she starred in were important pictures. Some of them are *Desert Fury* (1947) with Burt Lancaster, *Too Late for Tears* (1949), *The Company She Keeps* (1950), and *Scared Stiff* (1953) with Martin and Lewis and the late Carmen Miranda. Although Hal Wallis and Liz ended their contract in 1953 his office still gets fan mail and phone calls inquiring about her.

In 1953 the star was represented by attorney Jerry Giesler when she sued *Confidential* magazine, which was always being sued and settling out of court. The publication had carried an article by Matt Wilson that suggested Liz had known three call girls intimately. The story also repeated an interview she had given to columnist Sidney Skolsky some time before in which she stated that she always wore men's cologne and pajamas, and hated frilly, feminine dresses. The fact that Miss Scott had spent time in the company of Paris's famous lesbian entertainer, Frede, and had been drinking heavily, did not weigh in her favor.

Her later movies were *Silver Lode* (1954), *Loving You* (1957) with Elvis Presley, and her last, *The Weapon* (1957) for Republic Studios.

Lizabeth lives in the same apartment she occupied as a star, located at the residential end of Hollywood Boulevard. She is seen occasionally at a screenland party or driving around town in her open convertible. Infrequently a column item about her appears; last year one had her engaged to a William Dugger but to this day Liz has never been married. She has refused countless requests from interviewers, many of them sympathetic and genuinely interested in seeing her back on the screen. One casting director who talked to her recently found that she wanted to work again but that her requirements were "unrealistic." However, her very poor eyesight, which has become worse, may be behind it.

In the meantime, her distinctive good looks and voice have won her an entire new generation of fans who watch her in old films on television. She has recently been *heard* in television commercials for juice and cat food.

At a recent Hollywood party. *Jon Virzi*

A regular on the Eddie Cantor radio show, 1938.

THE MAD RUSSIAN: Bert Gordon

The dialect comedian was born Barney Gorodetsky in 1900 in Manhattan's Lower East Side. He debuted at the age of six singing soprano in a local synagogue. That same year he appeared at Kessler's Thalia Theatre, a Jewish theatre on the Bowery. By the time he was fourteen, Bert was part of Gus Edwards's Newsboy Sextette. Others in the act were Walter Winchell, Jack Weener, Georgie Price, and Bert Wheeler.* Bert also worked for Joe Woods in his "Nine Crazy Kids," an act not unlike Gus Edwards's famous "School Days" skit. Bert's first "teacher" in that act was Jack Pearl,* who was replaced by the late Bert Lahr.

Gordon worked a lot in vaudeville. His huge ears made him funny even before he opened his mouth. The various accents he had picked up from his neighborhood served him well in comedy routines as a German, Jew, Irishman, Russian, and so on. He worked mostly with luscious, statuesque show girls. His best, he says, was Jean Ford, who was his partner in an act called "Gordon and Ford." There was also "Gordon and Grey," "Bert Gordon and Florence Shubert," and "Bert Gordon and Alice Knowlot." For a time he worked with his brother Harry, who is now retired and living in Manhattan. In the early twenties he had an act called "Desperate Sam," which he maintains is the first western comedy ever presented in vaudeville.

The late George White cast him in his *Scandals of 1921* along with Ann Pennington,** the late Aunt Jemima, and Lou Holtz. The show ran for ninety-seven performances and was followed by a two-year tour of Europe. He appeared on Broadway in *Billy Rose's Crazy Quilt* (1931) with Fanny Brice and Ted Healy for sixty-seven performances.

Jack Benny introduced Bert into radio in the early 1930s, but he is best remembered for his association with the late Eddie Cantor. Bert first ap-

108

peared on Cantor's popular variety program in 1935, and a year later Bert introduced his famous character, "The Mad Russian," on the air. It was an instant success. Each week, his salutation, "How do you do?" in a thick Russian accent brought squeals of delight from studio audiences and stacks of mail asking for more appearances by the ridiculous Slav. Bert and Cantor worked together steadily until 1949, and they remained close friends until Cantor's death in 1964.

Bert worked in a number of movies. He costarred in *New Faces of 1937* for RKO with the late Joe Penner; Penny Singleton ** was with him in *Outside of Paradise* (1938) ; and *Laugh Your Blues Away* (1942) followed with Jinx Falkenberg (living in Manhasset, Long Island, with her husband, public relations executive Tex McCrary), who was also with him in *Sing for Your Supper* (1941). Bert's last feature was *Let's Have Fun* (1943) with Margaret Lindsay (who lives with Mary McCarty on Wellesly Drive, West Hollywood).

During this period he had returned to Broadway in 1940 to do the musical *Hold on to Your Hats,* which starred Al Jolson.

The 1950s brought an end to dialect comedians. Bert worked a few times on early television but there was little demand for his services. In 1964 Dick Van Dyke used him on his popular television series, and this appearance led to an engagement at Billy Gray's Band Box in Los Angeles. It was Bert's first job in a long time, and his last.

The Mad Russian lives alone in a small apartment on Beverly Boulevard; he was divorced in 1938 after thirteen years of marriage to Follies girl Edna Wheaton. They had no children. Bert suffers from bad eyesight and a partial hearing loss. He plays a good deal of bridge. During Christmas seasons he works for a business-gift firm, Hesco, Ltd., in Beverly Hills. He is still recognized by fans, especially by the older Jewish people on Fairfax Avenue in Los Angeles, and Bob Hope calls on him from time to time.

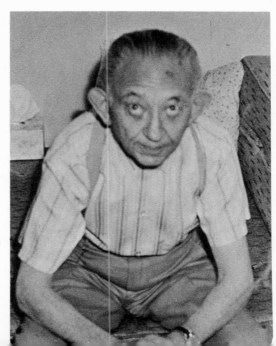

In his Beverly Boulevard apartment, Los Angeles. *John P. Gilligan*

Made up as Ma, 1946. *NBC Radio*

MA PERKINS: Virginia Payne

The popular radio character on daytime radio for twenty-seven years, heard twice daily, on two networks, not including Radio Luxembourg, was originated by Virginia Payne. The kindly old lady from "Rushville Center" was first heard on December 4, 1933, out of Cincinnati's WLW (the call letters standing for, according to some of the actors, World's Lowest Wages) .

Ma was Proctor and Gamble's first venture into network radio, and the original contract was for a trial of sixteen weeks. From the beginning, the serial was hugely successful, with letters pouring in from around the country with sales of Oxydol, the sponsor's product, soaring. Following the trial run, the show moved to Chicago where Murray Forbes essayed the role of Willie Fitz, husband to Ma's daughter Evey for the full series run. Only Forbes and Virginia were with the show from the outset. A second daughter, Fay Henderson, had three successive interpreters. When widowed Ma's only "son" John was killed during the war, she was deluged with wires and letters of sympathy. Virginia, hardly old enough to be married when she won the part, was often flooded with mail begging advice on personal problems.

The radio stories centered on the everyday problems of a grandmother who with the help of her old friend Shuffle Shober, played by Charles Egleston, ran a lumberyard in a small town. If Ma had less drama than other soaps, her troubles were more realistic. A constant thorn in her side was Evey, whom listeners considered "a heartache" to her mother. Evey was president of a ladies' club, The Jolly Seventeen, that thrived on gossip. Ma would have no truck with such things.

Ma was originally conceived as a raucous old woman not unlike Marie Dressler's role in the *Min and Bill* movie series. But Virginia Payne felt

110

that the "twinkle in Dressler's eye" could not be projected over radio and softened the character until she evolved a warm, tolerant person constantly at odds with the small-minded residents in the fictional town. *Variety* labeled her character "Just Plain Bill in drag."

With "Old Kentucky Home" playing softly in the background, the announcer would open each program with, "And now, Oxydol's own Ma Perkins . . ." After thirteen years in Chicago the series moved to New York where it continued for another thirteen. Listeners were so entranced that door-to-door salesmen knew better than to make calls during these fifteen-minute segments carried by NBC on both its Red and Blue networks.

When the serial went off the air in 1960, thousands of written and oral protests were received from loyal listeners. During the last broadcast, a re-creation of a Thanksgiving dinner at "Ma's House," the network's switchboard was jammed with callers who could hardly express their anger and sorrow for the tears they shed.

For Virginia Payne, the demise of Ma meant freedom to play onstage and in other radio and television shows, which she has done ever since. Even during the reign of Ma on the airways, Virginia worked for rival soaps and in such series as the *First Nighter*. Also, she has been a perennial favorite at Houston's famed Alley Theatre.

Virginia, now in her midfifties, is active in union affairs and is past president of AFTRA (American Federation of Television and Radio Artists) locals in Chicago and New York as well as the national president. She is unmarried and maintains an apartment on Manhattan's East Fifty-fifth Street and a summer home in Ogunquit, Maine. She is still frequently recognized by her voice, which a couple of years ago was used for radio commercials for apple juice under the guise "Apple Grannie." It was a shameless spoof.

The real Ma today. *Anselma Dell'Olio*

In 1940 on *Truth or Consequences.*

RALPH EDWARDS

The quizmaster of radio and television in the 1940s and 1950s was born on June 13, 1913, in Merino, Colorado. His mother, who was widowed when Ralph was still very young, owned and operated her own creamery there until her son was sixteen. At that time, the Edwards family moved to California.

Ralph sold his first radio script to an Oakland station for one dollar. Soon he was writing several a week at somewhat higher pay. Within a short time he was hired full time by the station, and managed to put himself through the University of Southern California.

After he got out of college in 1936, Edwards hitchhiked to New York City for a part in a Broadway show he had been promised. When he arrived, the show had already folded. For three months he slept in the Actor's Church and lived on health food. Then he was hired as an announcer at CBS Radio. His voice was heard on such programs as *Major Bowes Amateur Hour* and *The Gumps.* During his lean years in New York he shared an apartment with Andre Baruch (living with his wife, Bea Wain, in Scarsdale), and former Yankee sportscaster Mel Allen.

In 1940 Ralph took the old parlor game *Truth or Consequences* and made it into one of the most popular programs on radio. The show, which he hosted, was such a success that a small town in New Mexico took the title for its name, and Ralph's weekly query to the audience, "Aren't we devils?" became a common expression. Later in the forties he gathered a lot of publicity and upped his already high ratings when he introduced mystery personalities the radio audience could guess: His radio audience had to include in their letters a contribution to a charity. His "Miss Hush" (the late Clara Bow), "Mr. Hush" (Jack Dempsey), and "The Walking Man" (Jack Benny) were the subjects of speculation throughout the nation and raised over $6 million. The show moved to television and is still being produced, although Edwards was replaced by Bob Barker years ago.

Of shorter duration but equal success was his *This Is Your Life* series which was broadcast first in 1948 and moved to television on October 1, 1952, where it enjoyed huge popularity until it went off the air nine years later. On it, Edwards in his very gushy style fawned over such personalities as Gloria Swanson, Billy Graham, Jeannette MacDonald, and Dorothy Lamour. (His weekly subject was unaware that he was to be the topic of the program until it began and not all were completely happy about the surprise. Lowell Thomas was so angry right on camera that he returned later to apologize.)

Ralph appeared in several movies such as *Radio Stars on Parade* (1945) and *The Bamboo Blonde* (1946).

He not only created his own programs but he emceed and packaged them as well, reaping the profits of each role. He and his shows were the subjects of countless parodies and satires. Though Ralph realized the publicity value of such spoofs, they seldom amused him. About the only humor he ever exhibited about himself or his work was when he broke the tension during script meetings by removing his toupée with a flourish.

Edwards produced several other shows in the late fifties: *Place the Face, It Could Be You,* and *End of the Rainbow,* none of them a great success.

To the surprise of most who knew him in his heyday, Ralph has not only stayed off camera during the past decade but has interfered very little in the production of *Truth or Consequences.* The man who for years commanded a weekly audience of from 25 to 30 million lives quietly with his wife Barbara Jean, whom he married in 1939. They have homes in Beverly Hills and on the ocean in Malibu and "three little consequences": Chris, Gary, and Lauren. Ralph has been honored by his alma mater as the Alumnus of the Year and in 1967 was given the Carbon Mike Award by the Pacific Pioneer Broadcasters for having sold over $500 million in war bonds. He is active in Los Angeles civic affairs and spends a great deal of time hunting and fishing.

With Clark Kerr (left), former president of Ralph's alma mater, at an alumni dinner. *UPI*

With Lionel Barrymore in a scene from M-G-M's *Dr. Kildare's Crisis,* 1940.

LARAINE DAY

Dr. Kildare's girl friend was born in Roosevelt, Utah, in 1917. Her grand-father, who was a Brigham Young elder, has fifty-two children. Laraine was one of eight. Her father, a contractor, moved the family to Long Beach, California, when she was in the fifth grade. Later she attended high school there and joined a little theatre group called the Players Guild. Among the members was Robert Mitchum with whom she later costarred in *The Locket* (1946). A scout from Hollywood caught one of her performances and got her a job in Paramount's *Scandal Sheet* (1931), which starred the late Kay Frances and Clive Brook (who lives in Eaton Square in London). Laraine then returned to Long Beach and the Guild until an agent took her to Goldwyn studios, where she landed a tiny part in Barbara Stanwyck's classic version of *Stella Dallas* (1937).

She did several others at RKO with George O'Brien (now retired and widowed, living in Brentwood, California) under her real name, Laraine Johnson; Day was taken from Elias Day, the Guild director. M-G-M saw her, and she was tested for a role with Wallace Beery in *Sergeant Madden* (1939). She won the part and a contract with the studio where she was to become best known for the role of a nurse in the famed *Dr. Kildare* series, starring Lew Ayres. Laraine and Lew became one of the most popular couples on the screen. Fans flooded the studio with letters when Laraine was hit by a truck and died in her fifth and last episode. Her image of a nurse was so strong that Cecil B. De Mille, who had once said she had no talent whatsoever, hired her from Metro at a huge fee to play a nurse with Gary Cooper in *The Story of Dr. Wassell* (1944).

Laraine is none too happy with her films and feels that her best work was done away from her home lot. "They never really wanted me for any-thing. I was always the one who happened to be free when their first choice wasn't," she said recently. The only picture that she is pleased with from her Culver City days is *My Son, My Son* (1940); which starred Madeleine

Carroll,** and the only reason she won that role is that during the first week of shooting, Frances Dee, who had been cast in it, collapsed on the set.

Laraine avoided studio politics as well as dates the publicity department tried to set up for her with other players. For such reasons she was never among the "in" group at Metro. She costarred with Edward G. Robinson in *Unholy Partners* (1941), Shirley Temple in *Kathleen* (1941), Cary Grant in *Mr. Lucky* (1943), and Robert Young in *Those Endearing Young Charms* (1945), but has never been close with any of them. Few of her friends are associated with movies, none from the old days.

From 1942 to 1947 she was married to Ray Hendricks, a former singer. They adopted two children: Michele in 1944 and Chris in 1945. Immediately upon her divorce from Hendricks she flew to El Paso, Texas, and married Leo Durocher, then manager of the New York Giants. In 1950 Laraine had a fifteen-minute radio interview show on WPIX in New York preceding each Giants game, afterward doing a WMGM late-night interview show. In 1952 her book *Day with the Giants* was published.

She and Durocher were divorced in 1960, and Laraine married Michael Grilikhas, a television producer. They have two daughters, Dana, six years old, and Gigi, four years old. All live in a hillside house that is part of the Trusdale Estates of Beverly Hills.

Laraine would like very much to work again. Her last movie was *The Third Voice* in 1960. She thinks she was always more popular with the public than with the studios, and feels the same is true today. She was anxious to do the part won by Maureen Stapleton in *Airport* (1969) but the producer could not see her in the role. She knows finding work is not easy: "People think it is easy if you have a name to get a job. It isn't. Believe me, for every part that comes up for a woman my age there are at least two dozen former stars who are up for it and really want it."

She and her husband are trying to package a syndicated television talk show for Laraine to be called *Day by Day*. In the meantime she busies herself with her children and a for-friends-only boutique that she and her stand-in maintain at home.

With her children Gigi and Dana by the pool of their Beverly Hills home. *Anselma Dell'Olio*

Under contract to Fox in the early thirties.

CHARLES "BUDDY" ROGERS

America's Boyfriend was born in Olathe, Kansas, in 1904. His father was a judge and the editor of the local paper, the *Mirror*. Buddy's first stage appearance was in his high school's version of Booth Tarkington's *Clarence*. Buddy attended the University of Kansas and on weekends played in a little jazz band for ten dollars on Friday nights and twelve dollars Saturdays. He could play saxophone, drums, and trombone, and had always aspired to music rather than acting.

He was put under contract to Paramount, attending their acting school in Astoria, Long Island, and upon graduation appeared in *Fascinating Youth* (1926). Audience reaction to his good looks was very favorable, and the studio put him into *So's Your Old Man* (1926) with W. C. Fields and Alice Joyce. His most important silent pictures came later; *Wings* (1927) a super-spectacular, starring Richard Arlen * and the late Jobyna Ralston and Clara Bow, and one of the biggest successes of its time (rereleased by Paramount in 1969 with some sound added) and *Abie's Irish Rose* (1928) with the late Nancy Carroll and Bernard Gorcey, father of the late Leo Gorcey.

Privately, his most important role was in *My Best Girl* (1927). His leading lady was America's Sweetheart, Mary Pickford, undoubtedly the biggest star in the history of motion pictures. The two met for the first time on the set. Miss Pickford was then married to Douglas Fairbanks, Sr. Buddy and Mary, eleven years his senior, were married in 1936 and went off on a Hawaiian honeymoon with their friends the late Jeanette MacDonald and her husband Gene Raymond (semiretired and living in Bel Air, California, and still one of their closest friends). The press and much of the public gave the couple six months.

116

While Miss Pickford was seen less and less as talkies took over, Buddy's career prospered. But the publicity of their marriage was not the only reason. Though he never became the world's best actor, Rogers had an easy manner and came across with considerable charm, as in the movies *Safety in Numbers* (1930) with Virginia Bruce,** *Young Eagles* (1930) with Paul Lukas (retired in Palm Springs, California), *This Reckless Age* (1932), *Old Man Rhythm* (1935), *This Way Please* (1937), *Golden Hoofs* (1941), *Mexican Spitfire's Baby* (1941), and *Don't Trust Your Husband* (1948) with Madeleine Carroll.** In 1957 he appeared in *The Parson and the Outlaw* with Sonny Tufts.**

Buddy Rogers and Mary Pickford still live in one of the most famous residences in the world—Pickfair, in Beverly Hills. Until the last few years they were seen at various film festivals and cinema salutes to Miss Pickford. Of late, however, Buddy makes an appearance alone. They still entertain such old friends as Lawrence Gray (retired and living in Mexico City) and Richard Arlen,* who appeared with Buddy on a *Petticoat Junction* television segment in 1968.

Buddy plays a lot of golf and almost daily visits an office in Beverly Hills that handles the enormous holdings of Miss Pickford. In spite of their wealth, he drives a 1955 Thunderbird and has a very informal manner. The state of their marriage and Miss Pickford's health have been the subject of speculation in Hollywood for some time but nothing can be deduced from Buddy's manner or answers. "Of course" is about the frankest and most revealing reply he has ever made. It was in answer to the question did he and his wife miss the limelight. The devout Christian Scientist has nothing but upbeat things to say on any subject.

At home in Pickfair, in Beverly Hills. *Clifford May*

The organist in 1944. *NBC Radio*

ETHEL SMITH

The organist whose recording of "Tico-Tico" sold over one million records was born in Pittsburgh in 1910. Ethel Goldsmith (her real name) was graduated from Carnegie Tech, where she majored in music and language. (She speaks French, Portuguese, Spanish, Italian, and German.) Her instrument was the piano; her first job, the pit of the local legitimate theatre. Then a Shubert show that was playing Pittsburgh took Ethel with it on a twenty-eight-week tour of the United States. While in California, she was offered a job playing the organ, accompanying a singer at a movie studio, and to gain practice went to a local music store and offered to demonstrate theirs. Within a few days customers were gathering around her to listen, so proficient had she become. From then on she was booked as an organist.

Ethel's star rose in 1940. She had been working a four-week booking in Rio de Janeiro, paying one hundred dollars weekly, then her top salary. She had gone over well, and the management kept extending her engagement. But one night, while roaming around a tough section of Rio, she heard an interesting beat. It came from a combo that was playing in the back room of a "cheap dance hall." She entered and mixed with the musicians during their break and asked what they were playing. No one knew the name or the composer but they explained that the song had been played for many years in Argentina. From then on Ethel began playing it in her act in the arrangement she had made of it for the organ. Her audiences, mostly wealthy Argentinians and tourists, had never heard the tune and acclaimed it. If it hadn't been for Pearl Harbor, says Ethel, she might still be there. But when the war broke out everyone advised her to return. In no time after coming to New York "Tico-Tico" was a smash hit and Ethel was be-

118

sieged with offers to play her hit recording. Ethel, a strong personality on and off stage, and with a flair for showmanship, remained a name in show business even after "Tico-Tico" was no longer hot. She commanded large sums to appear at presentation houses and in such films as *Bathing Beauty* (1944) with Esther Williams,** *George White's Scandals* (1945), and *Cuban Pete* (1946) with Desi Arnaz.

In 1945 Ethel married Ralph Bellamy, who at the time was appearing on Broadway in *State of the Union,* and the couple lived in Ethel's Park Ven-dome apartment. In 1947 Bellamy walked out, stating that he had no inten-tion of paying his wife alimony. Ethel charged abandonment and claimed that he drank heavily, that he was moody, and would lock himself in his room. The organist said her husband became jealous when at their parties she received most of the attention. Bellamy contended that she had advised him to be home fifteen minutes after his final curtain or he would find the door locked.

Ethel never remarried and has no children. She lives alone amidst neigh-bors columnist Louis Sobol and singer Arthur Tracy.* She still practices her organ and a piano a good deal and has also become quite proficient on the guitar. But she is reluctant to play clubs anymore. She hates interviews and people who bring up "Tico-Tico" whenever her name is mentioned, but often laments that had she copyrighted the song, how very rich she would be today. However, Ethel has made enough to live very well and can con-centrate on acting if she prefers. In recent years she accepted several small parts in plays that would showcase her talent for character acting. Her work in a Franchot Tone–Theatre Four production received some favorable attention, and last year she had a brief run in an off-Broadway musical ver-sion of *Tom Jones.* She is planning to write a book on her experiences in Europe and South America and will call it "Abroad with an Organ."

As she looks today.

A headliner in 1948. *NBC*

DICK CONTINO

The teen-age accordionist whose career was ruined when he attempted to evade the draft was born in 1930 in Fresno, California, to a Sicilian-born butcher and a very ambitious mother. The Continos bought Dick, their first child, an accordion when he was three years old. His mother, Mary, believed her boy to be exceptional in every way and encouraged him to practice his instrument and study hard at school. At seventeen, already six feet tall, he entered Fresno State College but did not stay long. Dick felt that his real chance for success was with his music.

By now his parents had bought him a fifteen-hundred-dollar accordion, and when Horace Heidt ** brought his "Youth Opportunity Hour" to Fresno, Dick entered as a contestant with his rendition of "Lady of Spain." His prize was two hundred fifty dollars plus a chance to play in the quarter finals. Thirteen weeks later after topping all the others on the applause meter with "Bumble Boogie" he walked away with an additional seven hundred fifty dollars in prize money and a chance at the grand prize. In March 1948 Dick appeared on "Philip Morris Night with Horace Heidt" over NBC Radio, and was declared winner of the grand prize—five thousand dollars.

Dick Contino was well managed and promoted. NBC-TV filmed a television pilot in which he played his accordion, a piano, and a ukulele. It did not sell, but he became a regular guest on the top television shows and got star billing in nightclub appearances. He had the clean-cut good looks liked by older ladies. His publicity played up his closeness to his mother and father, which did not hurt the all-American-boy image that was being forged so well by his managers.

In 1951 he was earning as much as four thousand dollars a week when he was arrested on charges of draft evasion after he had failed to report for his induction. Dick claimed that he suffered from a mental condition since he was six years old and that he had been under the care of a psychiatrist for the last three years. His trouble, said a spokesman, was claustrophobia. The courts would hear none of it. Contino was sentenced to a six-month term in federal prison and fined ten thousand dollars. He was deluged with mail from former fans who expressed their contempt for a boy who had "shirked his duty." After his release from prison Dick spent twenty months in the army, much of it a tour of duty in Korea. He was discharged as a sergeant.

He never regained the popularity he had known for over three years, although it was not from lack of trying.

He dated actress Piper Laurie for a while and then married starlet Leigh Snowden, in 1956. Four months later, with a debt of $51,983, the Continos declared bankruptcy. In the settlement, he payed $8,000 in back taxes and $1,300 in gambling debts.

Dick and his wife, who has had no luck in pursuing a singing career, live in Tarzana, California. They have three children: Mary, twelve; Deidre, ten; and Peter, six.

During the past two years Dick has toured United States Army camps in Vietnam, Bangkok, and Thailand. He still works as a single but now sings as well, and he has tried to become an actor, without success. In the meantime he supports his family with occasional club dates in Houston, Toronto, and Reno.

Of his past troubles, Dick's mother says, "Dick was no different from these long-haired boys who won't go into the army these days. He was just ahead of his time. Today he'd be a hero to the kids." The fact is that today he would never have made stardom to begin with. As for his being a hero, a long-time friend of the Contino family said that they did not oppose war or military service, but the interruption of Dick's career. Had Contino been assured of a Special Services job and lots of publicity, his mother would have had him enlist and herself led his first parade.

A new, mod Contino. *Antoinette Lopopolo*

With RKO, 1946.

LINDA CHRISTIAN

The former screen darling of the tabloids was born Blanca Rosa Welter in Tampico, Mexico, in 1924. Her mother was of Spanish-French-German descent and her father, a petroleum engineer, was Dutch. The family moved about a great deal during Linda's childhood, settling for a time in Venezuela and South Africa.

She came to Hollywood in the mid-1940s, and under the sponsorship of Errol Flynn, whom she had met in Acapulco, tried to break into movies via modeling and introductions. She landed a contract with RKO, but in the six months she was with them she made only one appearance on celluloid, in which she said, "Yes, sir."

While modeling in a fashion show for Lilly Daché, who called her "the copper girl" because of her complexion, she caught the eye of Louis B. Mayer's secretary, who took her straight to the mogul's office. M-G-M put her under contract and gave her a part in the Ilona Massey * film, *Holiday in Mexico* (1946). She appeared in several films but never made it as a movie star. Two were *Green Dolphin Street* (1947), and *Tarzan and the Mermaids* (1948) with Johnny Weissmuller * while under contract to the Culver City lot. But her real forte was publicity. Few stars broke the headlines and columns the way Linda would during her peak years.

She spoke a number of languages fluently, was gorgeous, and seemingly lacking in taste. Her first Hollywood beau after Flynn was Turhan Bey, who had been going with Lana Turner. Tyrone Power, another Turner date, met her in Rome and asked her to marry him, which she did, in 1949, wearing a one-thousand-dollar dress while one thousand mounted police held back hordes of teen-agers. She gave the late star a statue of herself clad only in a towel around her waist. They had two daughters, Romina, born in 1949 (she married Italian pop star Al Bano, a rumored former lover of Linda's), and Taryn, born in 1953. When the marriage ended in divorce in 1955, her settlement exceeded $1 million. She was to receive a percentage of Powers's earnings for the next two years plus a 36-percent and a 40-percent interest in his *Mississippi Gambler* and *The Long Gray*

Line respectively. Also in 1955 there was litigation over gifts from millionaire Robert H. Schlesinger amounting to one hundred thirty-two thousand dollars. In 1957, plans to marry the Marquis Alfonso de Portago were announced. That May, while awaiting Linda, de Portago and ten spectators were killed when the car he was driving in a race crashed in Italy. The next year was one of her best. Her new boyfriend, Francisco "Baby" Pignatari, gave her a one-hundred-forty-thousand-dollar solitaire diamond and hired thirty pickets to circle Linda's hotel after she refused to run away with him. She bragged that Brazilian millionaire Dircen Fontonra was also mad about her but the gentleman pleaded innocence.

Tyrone Power had remarried, and when he died in 1958 his widow specifically asked Linda not to attend the funeral. Linda arrived, bearing a cross of flowers, with her two daughters and Tyrone's last letter to her, posed for photos, and prayed at his grave. Afterward, she contested his will and was awarded half a million dollars of his Lloyds of London insurance policy.

In March 1962 Linda married British actor Edmund Purdom, an ex-boyfriend from 1956, and in April 1963 she filed for divorce; the columns linked her with star Glenn Ford, but he denied it.

Linda has resided for some time in Rome. In March 1968 she entered a clinic there for treatment for a nervous breakdown. According to the newspapers, she had been found wandering the streets after throwing her dog from the window of her fourth-floor apartment. Five months later her engagement to a Dr. Atanasio Concopoulus was announced, but they never married.

In March 1969 Linda announced she would act as press agent for her daughter Taryn, who was described by one magazine as having "a lovely sense of repose and a thoughtful face very reminiscent of the early Ingrid Bergman." Taryn would have to look long and hard to find anyone with a greater knack for getting her name in print.

Strolling in Rome recently. *PIX*

With Universal, 1937.

JOEL McCREA

The handsome leading man in the movies of the thirties and forties was born in South Pasadena, California, in 1905. His first brush with movie stars was as a newsboy delivering papers to the famous Western actor William S. Hart. Joel attended Hollywood High School and went to Pomona College.

By 1920 he was a stunt man, even doubling for female stars while falling off a horse. McCrea is one of the very few stars to rise from the ranks of extras. Fans of silent films still catch a glimpse of him in such old pictures as the Garbo vehicle *Single Standard* (1929).

In 1929 things began to happen for him. He was seen in *Jazz Age* (1929) and then was hired by the father of his former high school friend Cecilia De Mille for a featured role in *Dynamite* (1929). Joel and Cecil B. De Mille formed a friendship that lasted until the latter's death in 1959, although they only made one other picture, *Union Pacific* (1939), together. McCrea was originally cast as the male star of De Mille's *Northwest Mounted Police,* but felt uncomfortable in the part and was replaced by Gary Cooper.

He was placed under contract to RKO and appeared in such pictures as *The Silver Horde* (1930), *Kept Husbands* (1931), *Most Dangerous Game* (1932), *Private Worlds* (1935), and *These Three* (1936), the screen adaptation of Lillian Hellman's play *The Children's Hour.* His performances were low-keyed and his screen personality was likeable, if not very distinctive. He became what is called in the movie industry "a dependable performer." It was his "everyman" image that made Alfred Hitchcock choose him for the male lead in the superb thriller *Foreign Correspondent* (1940). Some of his other films were *Wells Fargo* (1937), *Dead End* (1937) with Wendy Barrie (living in New York City) and, in the forties, when he really came into his own, *Sullivan's Travels* (1941), *The Great Man's Lady* (1942), *The Palm Beach Story* (1942), and *The More the Merrier* (1943). Then began his Western period, which he never really left: *The Virginian* (1946), an exceptionally good one; *Ramrod* (1947) with Veronica Lake,* *Four Faces West* (1948), *Colorado Territory* (1949), *Cattle Drive* (1951), *Wichita* (1955), *The Tall Stranger* (1957), *The Gunfight at Dodge City* (1959), and *Ride the High Country* (1962), his last feature film.

In the interim, in 1952 McCrea and three other Hollywood actors had formed Four Star Productions, which produced some of the early money-making series on television. Also, in 1959, he and his son Jody starred as Marshal Mike Dunbar and Deputy Ben Matheson on the television series *Wichita Town*.

Joel had close professional associations with several ladies: the late Constance Bennett, who for a time was also his constant companion, Barbara Stanwyck, and Frances Dee, whom he married in 1933. The two separated several years ago but canceled plans for a divorce when they realized the legal complications and financial considerations involved. They live on their huge ranch in Camarillo, California, with their teen-age third son, Peter. Their eldest boy, David, manages his father's ranch in Shandon, California. The second son, Jody, who has been enjoying a fairly active acting career, upsets his father who strongly disapproves of Jody's nearly exclusively male social life.

McCrea credits his astute business sense to what he learned from his old friend Will Rogers, who taught him real estate values. Recently Joel sold twelve hundred acres of ranch land near Moorpark, California for $1.3 million. He had purchased it in 1931 for nineteen thousand five hundred dollars.

Long interested in the plight of the American Indian, he will be seen in a 1970 documentary, *Sioux Nation* filmed in South Dakota at the Pine Ridge Sioux Indian Reservation.

On location for *Sioux Nation,* Pine Ridge, South Dakota, 1969.

The pert character actress in
1941. *M-G-M*

UNA MERKEL

The pert character actress was born in 1903 in Covington, Kentucky. Her
traveling salesman father took his family all over the South by horse and
buggy and by train. She was nine when she was finally put into school, in
Philadelphia; later, in New York, she was enrolled in the Alviene School of
Dance and studied dramatics with Tyrone Power's mother. She was older
now, and to help support herself she did modeling for magazines, usually
True Story, and worked as an extra in movies, many of which were made in
the East then. Because of her resemblance to Lillian Gish, she was signed
to play the star's sister in a picture, but for lack of funds it was never finished. Broadway producer John Golden, during an interview, found her
candor refreshing when she admitted her lack of experience, and gave her
a one-line part in *Two by Two* (1925), which was good for two weeks. Next
she went into *The Poor Nut*, written and acted by the Nugents, in which
she also had one line. That lasted three weeks. She was in *Pigs* for a year,
then Golden put her in the road company of that play, in which she also
understudied Nydia Westman. While on tour with *Pigs*, she was signed by
Jed Harris for a part in the Helen Hayes vehicle *Coquette*, which lasted
twenty-two months on Broadway before going on the road. Though nothing
came of it at the time, it also got her a screen test (along with two other
unknowns, Sylvia Sidney and Claudette Colbert).

Golden again cast her, this time in his *Two Girls Wanted*, and then in
The Gossipy Sex, playing the leading feminine role opposite that star, Lynne
Overman. Later, an agent at United Artists remembered her screen test
when D. W. Griffith was looking for a girl to play Ann Rutledge in his
Abraham Lincoln (which starred Walter Huston), and it was the beginning
of her Hollywood career.

Following her official film debut, she got a number of comedy roles, an appearance in *Private Lives* (1931), which starred Norma Shearer * and Robert Montgomery, and a contract with M-G-M. Una's performances in comedy soon got her typecast. She was just short of beautiful, with features somewhat perky and winsome. Her pictures for Metro included *Clear All Wires* (1933) with Lee Tracy; *Blonde Bombshell* (1933) with Jean Harlow; *Cat's Paw* (1934) with Harold Lloyd;** *It's in the Air* (1935) with Jack Benny; *Riff-Raff* (1936) with Jean Harlow and Spencer Tracy; *Saratoga* (1937) with Jean Harlow and Clark Gable; *Test Pilot* (1938) with Clark Gable and Myrna Loy; and *On Borrowed Time* (1939) with Lionel Barrymore.

Probably she is best remembered for *Destry Rides Again* (1939), in which she had a rough and tumble catfight with Dietrich that ended in a draw. But her best part was in *Summer and Smoke* (1961), for which she won an Academy nomination. (She had previously played the menacingly addled mother on the stage at the La Jolla Playhouse, in California.)

In 1944, after an absence of fifteen years, she returned to the New York stage to do *Three's a Family*, again working for John Golden. She also did *The Remarkable Mr. Pennypacker* in 1953 and *The Ponder Heart* in 1956. In 1959 she was in *Take Me Along*, the Broadway musical version of O'Neill's *Ah, Wilderness!*

Una was married to Ronald L. Burka, an aviation designer, in 1932. They were divorced in 1946. Twice her name made the front pages: in 1945, when her mother committed suicide by taking gas—nearly killing Una at the same time; and in 1952, when she nearly died from an overdose of sleeping pills.

Una and her father, who is in his nineties, live in an ultramodern apartment in Los Angeles. Says Una: "I most probably will work again some time, but I don't have to ever if I choose, so I am being mighty fussy."

At home in her Los Angeles apartment. *Peaches Poland*

During the forties, one of M-G-M's most popular, and most troublesome, stars.

ROBERT MONTGOMERY

The dapper star, director, producer, and critic of stage, movies, and television was born in Beacon, New York, in 1904. Before making his Broadway debut in *The Mask and the Face* (1924), he was a mechanic on a railroad and a deckhand on an oil tanker. He had received a good education in schools here and abroad but had to support himself after his father, an executive with a rubber company, died, leaving the family completely without money. After a stint in stock, Robert acted on Broadway in such plays as *Dawn* (1924), *One of the Family* (1926), *The Garden of Eden* (1927), and *Possession* (1928). In 1929 he and his life-long friend, Elliott Nugent, debuted in M-G-M's *So This Is College*. Robert was an immediate hit, judging from the fan mail, and it was the beginning of the battles he would wage with his studios throughout his Hollywood career, which ended in 1950 with his performance in *Eye Witness*. The front office was determined to typecast him as the debonaire young man in the white dinner jacket. Robert lamented that he could do more than play tennis and light cigarettes for leading ladies. The first time he really broke the image was in *Big House* (1930) when he played a disturbed killer. Seven years later he again dispelled the idea that his only forte was light comedy when he stole *Night Must Fall* from Rosalind Russell and Dame May Whitty in his portrayal of a mad murderer who carried around a hatbox containing a severed human head.

While turning in beautifully understated performances in such films as *When Ladies Meet* (1933), *Forsaking All Others* (1934), *Piccadilly Jim*

(1936), *The Earl of Chicago* (1940), *Here Comes Mr. Jordan* (1941), and *Ride the Pink Horse* (1947), Montgomery was also serving as president of the Screen Actor's Guild. In that position he brought the activities of labor racketeer Willy Bioff to the attention of the press. For a while in the forties he was a radio commentator.

Twice nominated for an Oscar for best actor, Montgomery also distinguished himself as a director in motion pictures and in television. His *Robert Montgomery Presents,* which lasted on NBC from 1950 to 1957, is still hailed as one of the finest dramatic programs television has ever produced. In it, he functioned as producer and, on occasion, star and director.

Since leaving television he has been a severe and constant critic of the medium. His book *An Open Letter from a Television Viewer* (1968) is a scathing indictment of the industry for its monopolistic tactics. Since its publication he has traveled around the country trying to persuade his fellow citizens that radio and television are owned, controlled, and censored not only by the networks but by the politicians who own and represent stations. He has accused CBS President Frank Stanton of "double-talking" on the matter of educational public television, and he appeared before a congressional committee to decry the situation. The only important talk show that allowed him to appear was *Tonight,* which promptly censored some of his remarks.

From 1928 to 1950 he was married to actress Elizabeth Allan (who lives in Patterson, New York). After their divorce he married Elizabeth Harkness. They maintain an apartment in Manhattan but travel a great deal. Robert is on the boards of several large corporations and is one of the directors of Lincoln Center for the Performing Arts. He is delighted with the success of his daughter, Elizabeth, in television but says he had no interest in acting again.

In his office these days in Manhattan's Squibb Building. *Anais Aiken*

Myrt (left) and Marge, 1932.

MYRTLE (MYRT and MARGE) VAIL

The costar of America's popular dramatic radio show *Myrt and Marge,* was born in Joliet, Illinois, in 1888. At seventeen she was one of Ned Washburn's "Broilers," a line of beauties who appeared around the country in his show "The Umpire." Two years later, in 1907, she married the show's leading man, George Damerel, a prominent actor of his day, who gave her a daughter, Donna, the following year. In 1912 they rejected a movie contract that then went to Francis X. Bushman and Beverly Bayne.** In 1924 "Damerel & Vail & Co." changed the name of their act to "The Three of Us" as Donna joined her parents. They toured the Orpheum and Keith circuits, and for a time George played Prince Danilo in the Chicago company of *The Merry Widow.* In 1925 a serious depression hit vaudeville as silent movies came into their own, and the Damerels settled in Chicago. George went into the real estate business and Donna began working as a chorine at the old Rainbow Gardens. Then came the 1929 crash, by 1930 they were flat broke, and George was quite ill.

That next summer Myrtle conceived the idea of a radio series about two sisters and their lives in show business. She would play the older part, a hard-boiled but good-hearted trooper always on the lookout for the well-being of her little sister, Marge. Myrtle wrote ten scripts and took them to the Wrigley chewing gum people, and together they worked out a show. To the theme "Poor Butterfly," the program went on the air November 2, 1931. It was an immediate hit, and in 1932 Mayor Jimmy Walker presented her with the New York *Mirror* award for the most popular dramatic show on radio. It was heard on CBS opposite NBC's *Amos 'n' Andy* until 1936, but beginning with the 1937 season, the show switched to a daytime slot, and continued to emanate from Chicago. For a time the show was so popular that they had to do two broadcasts a day to coincide with the different time zones.

In 1941 Donna—then married to her third husband, Peter Fick—died giving birth to a boy, Donnie, and Marge was taken over by Helen Mack (who lives next door to Lanny Ross * on Manhattan's East Fifty-seventh Street). In 1942 the show was dropped.

There was the usual cry of outrage from loyal fans and industry talk of its return continued for years. In 1949 a television pilot was made, which Myrtle recalls was "a mess," but it never sold.

During its time, the show helped spawn some interesting careers: Cliff Arquette (Charlie Weaver to television watchers) got his start playing the character Thaddeus Cornfelder, and others were Dave Garroway, Tyrone Power, Del Sharbut, Ralph Edwards, Raymond Johnson and the late Ed Begley.

Myrtle Vail never remarried after her husband died in 1936. After living in California, New Jersey, and, for a time, Europe, she moved to Chicago. She has a son, George, a businessman in Kansas City, Missouri, and grandchildren through Donna. Occasionally she guests on a Chicago radio or television station "for free," and she has done comedy bits in *Bucket of Blood* (1959) and *The Little Shop of Horrors* (1958), both American-International cheapies.

Notwithstanding her battle with cataracts, Myrtle occupies herself reading the books she once had no time for. She still owns all rights to *Myrt and Marge* and has been working on an updated version for television. She refuses to say if in the new treatment she will again be the Captain of the Chic Chicks, a line of twenty-four crack dancers performing in what must be one of the longest-running shows, fictional or otherwise, in history: "Hayfield's Pleasures," the show within a show that held radio audiences captive for nearly twelve years.

Myrt and son George on her eighty-first birthday. *Kermit Kelly*

In 1948, the year he went independent.

JOHN PAYNE

The popular movie lead of the thirties and forties was born in Roanoke, Virginia, in 1912. His granduncle had preceded him in fame as the composer of "Home Sweet Home" though his father, a gentleman farmer, had less to sing about; he lost all his money in the stock-market crash of 1929. John attended Mercerberg Academy, Pennsylvania, Roanoke College, Virginia, and finally, in New York, Juilliard and Columbia where he studied voice and drama. During school months he supported himself with jobs in radio and toured in Shubert shows in the summer. For a while he had his own fifteen-minute radio program on WNEW.

In 1935 he was stand-in for the late Reginald Gardiner in *At Home Abroad*, a Bea Lillie musical with Ethel Waters ** and Eleanor Powell ** in the cast. A talent scout saw John one night when he took over for an ailing Gardiner and brought him to Hollywood, where he was put under contract to Sam Goldwyn. In his first and only year with Goldwyn he made *Dodsworth*, with the late Ruth Chatterton and Walter Huston, went to Paramount for a year, and then to Warner Bros., who used him as a threat to Dick Powell. Powell rejected the Busby Berkeley musical *Garden of the Moon* (1938) and John got the part. When his Warner Bros. contract expired he went to Twentieth Century-Fox.

By changing studios, while working constantly, Payne somehow managed to resist being typecast. He could play a boxer, a cowboy, or a tough guy and still be right at home in the Alice Faye, Sonja Henie,* or Betty Grable musicals. He had a good singing voice and was an excellent horseman.

Some of his features were *Tin Pan Alley* (1940), *Sun Valley Serenade* (1941), *To the Shores of Tripoli* (1942), *Wake Up and Dream* (1946), and *Sentimental Journey* (1946). He had bought the short story from which *Journey* was made from a magazine and sold it to Fox, but they promptly offered the lead to Cary Grant. Fortunately, Payne had cornered Darryl

132

Zanuck in the men's room and demanded a chance to test. After *Journey* he made *Miracle on 34th Street* (1947), *The Saxon Charm* (1948), and *Slightly Scarlet* (1956). Three years earlier, John had produced, coscripted, and starred in *The Boss,* a fine tight, low-budget dramatization of the career of political boss Thomas (Tom) Joseph Pendergast. Some people at the State Department thought it "not characteristic of the American society," it was denied a release abroad, and got very poor bookings in the United States. It is Payne's proudest effort and his one financial failure.

John had gone independent in 1948 with his Window Productions, setting up separate deals with Universal and Paramount. His 1957 *Restless Gun* television series was a big hit and still plays throughout the world. Most of that money went to John.

An accident in 1961 nearly killed him. He was struck by a car and knocked through the windshield. A team of doctors worked on him for six and a half hours and today there is hardly a sign of the surgery on his face. Although he had not made a feature film or television appearance since, in 1964 he toured in Meredith Wilson's *Here's Love,* and hated every minute of it.

Since 1953 Payne has been married to his third wife, Sandy Curtis, whose many paintings hang in their large house facing the Pacific. His first wife was Anne Shirley (now Mrs. Charles Lederer of Beverly Hills), his second, Gloria De Haven (now the hostess of a morning movie on New York's Channel 7). Shirley gave him a daughter, Linda, and De Haven gave him Tommy and Kathy.

John has little interest in acting, though he might be tempted by some good character parts. His time these days is spent developing scripts he has optioned or written. As early as 1954 John had recognized the potential of the James Bond character and had the rights to Ian Fleming's *Moonraker* sewed up in perpetuity. He offered *Moonraker* to major studios only to be told that it was "too violent, too sexy." Eventually he gave up on the project that became one of the biggest moneymaking ventures in motion pictures.

In his ocean-front home today in Santa Monica. *Diana Keyt*

A 1937 publicity still for *She Had to Eat*.

ROCHELLE HUDSON

The lovely ingenue and leading lady of the movies in the 1930s and 1940s was born in Oklahoma City, Oklahoma, in 1915. She began taking dancing lessons when only three years old, and when her family moved to Los Angeles in 1928, Rochelle began studying with Ernest Belcher, father of Marge Champion and stepfather of Lina Basquette. Belcher felt she had singing potential as well and sent her to the voice coach of Fox studios, where she was placed under contract.

At the time, production head Winifred Sheehan was squabbling with Janet Gaynor ** and Rochelle was hired as a threat to the star. For the six months that she was under contract she did nothing but go to school and take various lessons. All sets were closed and she met no one of any importance to her career. But when Fox dropped her option, director Frank Borzage gave her a screen test and she was placed under contract to RKO, where she made her first film *Are These Our Children?* (1931) with Eric Linden (married and living in South Laguna, California) . This was followed with *She Done Him Wrong* (1933) , *Imitation of Life* (1934) , *Les Miserables* (1935) , *Poppy* (1936) with W. C. Fields, *Born Reckless* (1937) with Brian Donleavy (who divides his time between Palm Springs and Los Angeles, *Convicted Woman* (1940) with June Lang (living with her daughter in North Hollywood, California) , *The Stork Pays Off* (1941) with Maxie Rosenbloom (living in a hotel in Hollywood) , *Bush Pilot* (1947) with Jack La Rue (ailing at the Motion Picture Country House in Woodland Hills, California) , and *Rebel Without a Cause* (1955) with James Dean.

By her own admission Rochelle was a "square peg in a round hole" in Hollywood. While being interviewed in New York during the time Fox was promoting her as a sweet young thing, she was asked about her home town, Claremont, Oklahoma (the studio publicity department thought it would be better copy to have her come from Will Rogers' birthplace) . Said the pretty actress to the reporter, "It stinks!" She was referring to its famed mineral baths. Claremont disowned her. Women's clubs throughout the country threatened to ban her films and the studio was beside itself.

She claims that she was just enough younger than Loretta Young so that the latter got the mature roles Rochelle wanted. "They kept me sweet and innocent for years. When I finally convinced them I was no longer a teen-ager I was immediately cast as a chippy, which I remained until I quit."

In 1950 she played Bonnie with Bert Lahr in *Burlesque* onstage and was seen in *That's My Boy* on television during the 1954–1955 season. Her only three pictures since *Rebel Without a Cause* were *Strait-Jacket* (1964) with Joan Crawford, *The Night Walker* (1964), and *Dr. Terror's House of Horrors* (1965).

During World War II she was married to Harold Thompson, a naval reservist. Together they made several trips to and from Mexico on the pretext of fishing expeditions. Actually they were engaged in espionage for the United States government. On one trip while accompanied by George Vanderbilt they discovered a large cache of high-test aviation gas hidden by German agents in Baja, California.

Her first marriage ended in divorce in 1947 and her second husband, Richard Hyland, was divorced in 1950. For the past eight years Rochelle has been the wife of a hotel executive.

In 1969, Rochelle moved from Hollywood to Palm Desert, California, where she has her own real estate brokerage office. Among her neighbors are Busby Berkeley, Irene Rich,* and Laura La Plante.** The only one she visits from her days in movies is Alice Faye, who resides in Palm Springs nearby.

Rochelle was immortalized a few years ago in an off-Broadway revue with a campy song entitled "The Rochelle Hudson Tango." Arthur Treacher often mentions her on the *Merv Griffin Show*, although the two haven't seen each other in years. Rochelle, however, says it would take a very good, well-paying part to get her to Hollywood again. Asked recently about Claremont she replied, "I knew the town well since my grandparents lived there. I've even been back since, and I want the world to know that Claremont still stinks!"

In her real estate office in Palm Desert, California. *Clifford May*

As Geronimo in *Broken Arrow,* 1950.

TONTO: Jay Silverheels

Tonto, as he was known to kids all over the world in the 1950s, was born the son of a Mohawk chief on an Indian reservation in 1920 in Ontario, Canada. As a boy, Jay excelled in athletics and was a local star at lacrosse, the Canadian national game. When still in his teens, he left his home to travel about North America, supporting himself in boxing and wrestling matches.

By 1938 he had risen in the ranks of the amateurs to the point where he was accepted as a contestant in the famed Golden Gloves competition. Jay entered in the middleweight class and emerged as the runner-up to the winner of that year's bouts.

After the war, Jay made his way to Hollywood, where the studios were offering many roles to young Indians in the westerns that were being made on an assembly-line basis. In his first feature he had not only a speaking part but screen billing in the part of Coatl, a Mexican-Indian, in *Captain from Castile* (1947) which starred Tyrone Power. Some of his other pictures were *The Prairie* (1947), *Key Largo* (1948), *Fury at Furnace Creek* (1948) with Victor Mature,** *The Pathfinder* (1952) with Elena Verdugo (living in Los Angeles), and *Yankee Buccaneer* (1952). Probably his best work was in the role of Geronimo in the James Stewart–Jess Chandler Western *Broken Arrow* (1950).

Silverheels is most closely identified with fiction's most famous Indian, Tonto, the faithful companion of the lone masked rider of the West—the Lone Ranger. Jay played the part in the television series from 1948 to 1961. The role, however, was quite restricted by the writing and direction. There were far more riding and stunts involved than acting.

Before *The Lone Ranger* series, he was typecast as an Indian. But thereafter he was typecast as a *particular* Indian. He ended up with so firm an image in the minds of the public and casting directors that he has found little work since. Even his having changed very little physically since then has kept him closely identified with a part he hasn't played in ten years.

The changing attitude in the United States toward Indians has somewhat hindered him also. Many feel that the Tonto part was equivalent to an Uncle Tom. Tonto may have taken as many chances as the masked white man, and addressed him as "Quimo Sabe," ("faithful friend"), but throughout the episodes, Tonto was always subservient as the "faithful Indian companion."

After 1961, Clayton Moore, who played the Lone Ranger, retired to Minneapolis, Minnesota. Jay, who had made two features with him, *The Lone Ranger* (1956) and *The Lone Ranger and the Lost City of Gold* (1958), continued his acting career in Hollywood. In 1961 Jay had a brief featured role on the CBS series *Frontier Circus,* and he has made occasional appearances on the *Mike Douglas Show, Pistols and Petticoats,* and *Gentle Ben.*

Jay lives with his wife of Italian descent in their home in Conoga Park, California, part of the San Fernando Valley. They have been married twenty-five years and have two boys and a girl. He supplements his acting income with work as a salesman and spends much time at the Indian Actors Workshop. Jay works closely with the annual All-American Indian Exposition, which displays Indian arts, crafts, and ceremonies. On several of his television appearances he has read some of his poetry, which is strongly influenced by his life as a boy on the reservation.

As Tonto in his last movie *The Phynx,* 1970. *Warner Bros.–7 Arts*

With her award from the World Film Festival for her performance in *Rope of Sand*, 1949.

CORINNE CALVET

The sultry French sexpot was born in Paris in 1925. Her nobleman father insisted that she change her surname when she became an actress. Her family name is Dibos, which is Basque.

Before going into the theatre, Corinne studied criminal law for a while at the Sorbonne. She doesn't agree that it was as radical a switch as most people think, saying, "A lawyer needs exactly what an actor needs, strong personality, persuasive powers, and a good voice."

She worked in *We're Not Married Yet* (1945), which starred Claude Dauphin, and then began working in the French theatre. She soon came to the attention of Paramount and was signed by their New York office. When she arrived in Hollywood she found there was a strong rivalry between the New York and Hollywood offices, and that she was resented on the West Coast. Immediately they set forth to change her completely. She had worn very little makeup and her hair was straight but hours in the makeup department produced the overgroomed, overpainted, overdressed sex symbol that the movie public came to know. Her screen test was "hysterical," she says today. Her option was dropped immediately and she then tested for M-G-M. They were not enthusiastic, but Hal Wallis, an independent producer, was. He signed her to a contract and brought her back to Paramount, where the same publicists, photographers, and makeup people who told her she would never make it were instructed to make her glamorous and famous.

Corinne debuted with Burt Lancaster in *Rope of Sand* (1949), a brutal but successful picture. Among the seventeen she has made to date are, *On the Riviera* (1951) with Danny Kaye, *What Price Glory* (1952), *Flight to Tangier* (1953), *So This Is Paris* (1954) with Gene Nelson (now a television director) and Gloria De Haven, *The Plunderers of Painted Flats* (1959) with the late Edmund Lowe, *Bluebeard's Ten Honeymoons* (1960), *Hemingway's Adventures of a Young Man* (1962), starring Richard Beymer (now directing movies in England), and *Apache Uprising* (1966).

Most of Corinne's time, when not making pictures, seems to have been devoted to her love life. She is in the process of divorcing her fifth husband. "I love him still, but then I love all of them still," she says. But she has other interests, too. She has completed a course at UCLA on the history of the religions of the world. Last year, she and her teen-age son, Robin, moved from Hollywood to an apartment on West End Avenue in Manhattan, and she has decorated her living room with the oil paintings she has done over the years.

She claims that for the first time in her life she is neither married nor involved with anyone, and finds it very much to her liking. "I went to a party alone for the first time ever recently," she said, "and after getting over the trauma of not having an escort, I found myself surrounded by attractive young men. It was very agreeable. I didn't have to worry if my date was flirting with someone else while I was flirting with someone else."

Turned on today. *Tina Esseks*

In a scene from the 1941 picture *Sign of the Wolf*.

MANTAN MORELAND

The pop-eyed comic was born in 1902 in Louisiana country where Mantan, derived from Cajun, is a common name. When he was in grade school he found that by merely rolling his eyes he could break up the class with laughter. His friends nicknamed him Google-Eyes.

The first chance Mantan had to escape the poverty all around him came when he was fourteen—he ran away with a carnival. He was soon apprehended and returned home. Shortly afterward he took off again, this time with a medicine show but again he was retrieved. He made it the third time: he donned a United States Army uniform to make him look older.

For a while Mantan traveled with the Higgenback and Wallace Circus. When he wasn't working he traveled about the country on a freight train. In Cleveland, Jimmy Cooper put him into a black-and-white review. He began to work a lot on the black vaudeville circuit, an entertainment medium almost completely unknown to white people.

During a trip to New York Mantan met the late Tim Moore, who many years later was to become a television star as the Kingfish on *Amos 'n' Andy*. In 1932 the two were teamed in an all-black review called *Yeah, Man,* which quickly folded. In 1936 Mantan found himself stranded in Long Beach, California, when the company manager of his show ran off with the receipts and salaries. He made his way to Hollywood and got a part in the Joe Louis picture *Spirit of Youth* (1937). Over ninety features followed, including *Tell No Tales* (1939), *Star Dust* (1940) with Charlotte Greenwood (a Christian Scientist living in Beverly Hills), *King of the Zombies* (1941), *Phantom Killer* (1942) with Joan Woodbury (a Palm Springs resident),

Palm Beach Story (1942), *Cabin in the Sky* (1943), and *Chip Off the Old Block* (1944) with Peggy Ryan. He is probably best remembered for the dozens of films he made as Charlie Chan's chauffeur and for the Frankie Darro films, both made at Monogram.

Along with his Hollywood films and appearances on the *Bob Burns Show* and with Rudy Vallee on radio, Moreland turned out some hysterically funny features made with blacks for black audiences. The Ted Toddy productions such as *Mantan Messes Up* (1946) and *Mantan Runs for Mayor* (1946) were big hits in theatres in the black neighborhoods in the forties.

In 1958 his career, greatly slowed by the changing attitude toward blacks on the screen, was brought to a complete halt when he suffered a serious stroke. He was not seen on the screen again until he brought the house down with a single, silent "take" in *Enter Laughing* (1967). In 1970 he appeared as the counterman in *Watermelon Man* with Godfrey Cambridge. Mantan feels that he is completely recovered from his stroke and is very anxious to work again.

Perhaps his funniest routines are what he called "indefinite talks," a nonsensical series of interruptions he and the late Benny Carter borrowed years ago from the team Flornoy and Miller. His partner today is Roosevelt Livingood, who in 1939 as a little boy saw Mantan in *One Dark Night* and made him his hero. The partners have appeared on such shows as Merv Griffin's and Bill Cosby's. Occasionally he works with his old friend Moms Mabley, and there is serious talk of the two doing a television series together.

Mantan lives in Los Angeles but comes to New York at least once a year for a visit with his wife of seventeen years. They have no children.

His highest salary in movies was $1,750 weekly, second only to Stepin Fetchit * among black entertainers of the day. Mantan spent every cent, and then some.

With partner Roosevelt Livingood in their Hollywood apartment. *Clifford May*

Lana Turner and Cheryl escorted by her father, Stephen Crane, after the girl ran away from school, 1957. *UPI*

CHERYL CRANE

Movie star Lana Turner's daughter and slayer of mother's lover Johnny Stompanato was born in 1944. Lana had married then-actor Stephen Crane in 1942 but the marriage was annulled shortly thereafter. The couple remarried when Lana found she was pregnant with Cheryl. Crane was her second husband; they were divorced in 1944.

Cheryl first made the papers in 1957 when she ran away from boarding school. The public knew little of the girl who was never featured in her mother's publicity. By this time Cheryl's father had left the acting profession and was the proprietor of the Luau, one of Beverly Hills's most fashionable restaurants and a gathering place of the stars.

After the night of April 5, 1958, Cheryl Crane was almost as famous as her mother. Lana, who was then thirty-seven, was having a torrid affair with a handsome hoodlum-type ex-marine named Johnny Stompanato. He had been arrested once for vagrancy and again for suspicion of robbery. The latter charge was dropped for lack of evidence. He had been married and divorced three times and was by five years Lana's junior. Stompanato was a known associate of the late Bugsy Siegel and had been Mickey Cohen's bodyguard. Lana had met him in London, where she was making a movie.

The official version of the scandal is that Cheryl and her mother were talking together in Cheryl's bedroom in Beverly Hills when Stompanato came in and started yelling at Lana, who claims she had been trying to break off their relationship for some time. Lana told her lover not to argue in front of her daughter, and the two went into the star's all-pink bedroom where a heated

142

argument ensued. Cheryl claims to have heard Stompanato threaten her mother. She says he yelled, "I'll get you if it takes a day, a week, or a year. I'll cut you up. If I can't do it myself I'll find someone who can." Cheryl ran downstairs and got a knife from the kitchen, ran back upstairs and, as she entered her mother's room, said, "You don't have to take that, Mother!" With that, she made a lunge, running the eight-inch blade into Stompanato's stomach.

Lana phoned her mother and asked her to call a doctor. Cheryl called her father. Lana then telephoned Jerry Giesler, the late crack trial lawyer. Someone at some point thought to phone the police. Stompanato was pronounced dead at the scene.

Lana's statement was, "I didn't know what was happening. I thought she was just poking Johnny with her finger." Cheryl pleaded, "I had to protect my mother. I thought he was going to get her."

Because she was a minor, the case never was brought to trial. Instead, Cheryl was sent to the El Retiro Country Home for Problem Girls, located in the San Fernando Valley and encircled by a twelve-foot wall. The judge had made her a ward of the supreme court of California. In 1960 Cheryl and two other girls scaled the wall and escaped. Four days later she phoned her father and was returned to El Retiro. She was released January 21, 1961, still a ward of the court, but with permission to live with her mother.

Few cases have inspired so much speculation by both press and public. There was even a film, *Where Love Has Gone*, 1964, that was a thinly veiled fictional version of the crime. Whatever really happened that night, no contradictory evidence or testimony has ever surfaced.

Her mother has since remarried, several times, and to date remains so. Cheryl does not live with either parent, and has remained single. When seen in public, she is usually in the company of girls. Now and then she appears at a Hollywood party or premiere, but she avoids the limelight and does not grant interviews. Recently Cheryl was detained by Los Angeles police when they noticed three half-grown marijuana plants in the back seat of her car. She is a hostess in one of her father's restaurants but most of the patrons she seats at the fashionable watering hole have no idea who she is.

At a recent Hollywood opening. *Jon Virzi*

Berkeley and a black-faced
Eddie Cantor on the set of
Roman Scandals, 1933.

BUSBY BERKELEY

The great choreographer of stage and screen was born William Berkeley Enos
in Los Angeles in 1895. His mother had acted in movies and on stage with
Alla Nazimova. His father, who was a director with Tim Frawley's stock
company, gave him the name Busby after a leading lady of the time, Amy
Busby.

In 1898 the Enos family moved to New York City. Busby attended a military academy and upon graduation took a job with a shoe company. During
World War I he served as a lieutenant in the 312th Field Artillery, 79th Division, and was General John J. Pershing's entertainment officer at Chau-
mont, France, and, later, in Germany. After leaving the army, he got a small
part in a Broadway show directed by John Cromwell, an old friend. He did
several other small parts and then started directing in stock. When he was
assigned his first musical, a choreographer had to be brought in because
Busby knew nothing about dancing. However, not long after, Berkeley was
Broadway's top dance director. Throughout the twenties in such shows as
Vanities of 1928 he defied those who were fond of saying that nothing much
that was new could be done with dancing. Before going to Hollywood he
had choreographed twenty-one shows, some of his successes being *A Connecticut Yankee* (1927), *Rainbow* (1928), and *Sweet and Low* (1930).

Film critic Dwight MacDonald's choice for Samuel Goldwyn's chief contribution to the American cinema is Goldwyn's bringing Busby to Hollywood in 1930 to stage the production numbers for such Eddie Cantor vehicles as *Whoopee* (1930), *Palmy Days* (1931), *Kid from Spain* (1932), and
Roman Scandals (1933). When Mary Pickford made her sole appearance in
a musical, *Kiki* (1931), Berkeley created the dances.

Berkeley is probably best remembered for his Warner Bros. period when
he staggered both the front office and the audiences in the depression days of
America by using one hundred lighted violins played by one hundred lus-

cious girls in *Gold Diggers of 1933* and one hundred grand pianos for the "Lullaby of Broadway" number in *Gold Diggers of 1935*.

To this day such old films as *Dames* (1934), *Gold Diggers of 1937*, *Babes in Arms* (1939), *Babes on Broadway* (1941), and *Girl Crazy* (1943) are shown at retrospective festivals, college campuses, and cinema clubs just for the sequences he directed. His "Berkeley top shot" and the kaleidoscope effect he achieved are subjects of study in university motion-picture departments. At the time, his work was praised for its lavishness and extravagance, but now directors are awed that he accomplished all this with only one camera, very few retakes, and little editing. Even those unfamiliar with movie techniques are delighted by his old films on the late show. College kids pack his festivals to "groove on Berkeley's camp," and choreographers and directors admit the near impossibility of staging a large dance number without borrowing something from Busby Berkeley. Even during his heyday, directors copied him shamelessly.

Among his last movies were *Cinderella Jones* (1946), *Two Weeks with Love* (1950), *Easy to Love* (1953), and *Jumbo* (1962).

During the past five years Busby Berkeley has been honored at retrospective shows of his work in Paris and London, as well as at locations throughout Scandinavia and South America. Berkeley and Ruby Keeler, the actress he made a star, have been making personal appearances all over the world. When in 1965 the Huntington Hartford Gallery of Modern Art presented "A Tribute to Busby Berkeley," they had to turn away hundreds of patrons every day, and all during some of New York's worst weather in years. The program was so successful that it was repeated a year later, again to packed houses daily. To the surprise of all, the audiences were comprised primarily of young men and women born at least ten years after Berkeley's early work.

Berkeley and his sixth wife, Etta, live in Palm Desert, California. Buz has created several television commercials during the past couple of years. When producers decided to stage a revival with Ruby Keeler, of the 1925 musical *No, No, Nanette* in the fall of 1970, they signed as director The Master Builder of the American Film Musical, Busby Berkeley, who never had a dance lesson in his life.

A brief appearance in the film *The Phynx*, 1970. *Warner Bros.–7 Arts*

The "girl-next-door," 1944.

JUNE HAVER

The Girl Next Door known to millions of moviegoers in the 1940s was born June Stovenour in Rock Island, Illinois, in 1926. Her father, who had once played with John Philip Sousa's band, died and June's mother married Bert Haver, a draftsman. When she was six years old June made her debut, on stage, at the Cincinnati Suburban Theatre in *Midnight in a Toyshop*. The following year she won first prize in the Cincinnati Conservatory of Music Poet-Music contest—a solo piano appearance with the Cincinnati Concert Orchestra conducted by Eugene Goossens. At eight, she was offered a screen test, which her mother declined, explaining that she wanted her daughter to have a normal childhood. June studied drama at the Little Theatre at Mariemont and the Schuster-Martin School, and at nine won the annual oratory contest at Hamilton Carnegie Public School. The next year her family moved back to Rock Island, where June sang at a school opening and won a spot on a local radio program. By eleven, she had her own radio show, sponsored by an ice-cream company in which she sang, emceed, and played piano for two dollars a week.

At thirteen, June was soloist with Dick Jurgens's orchestra and then went with Freddie Martin. By the time she was fifteen, she and her mother were touring with Ted Fio Rito and his band, which took them to Hollywood. While there, she made two shorts for Universal, one with Rito, the other with Tommy Dorsey. The rest of the Havers came out to join them, and June enrolled at Beverly Hills High School, where she was voted the most talented student and won first prize in an interscholastic debate. She played the lead in the high school production of *Ever Since Eve*. A talent scout from Twentieth Century-Fox spotted her and signed her to a contract, but it stipulated that she be allowed to finish the school term. Later, her option was not picked up because the studio thought she looked too young. But in less than a year, in 1943, she was signed again by the studio.

Her image was of a sweet young thing, and her pictures were perfect examples of the period's slick, glossy musicals. June was groomed to succeed Fox's Betty Grable, who had replaced Alice Faye at the Fox lot. But though June was prettier than Betty Grable and considerably softer, she lacked a strong screen personality. Some of her pictures were *Home in Indiana* (1944), which starred Lon McAllister (retired and living in Venice, California), *Irish Eyes Are Smiling* (1944) with Dick Haymes,** *Where Do We Go from Here* (1945) with Joan Leslie,* *The Dolly Sisters* (1945), *Three Little Girls in Blue* (1946), *I Wonder Who's Kissing Her Now?* (1947) with Mark Stevens (now the tennis instructor at a hotel on Mallorca, Spain), *Scudda Hoo! Scudda Hay!* (1948), *The Daughter of Rosie O'Grady* (1950), *Love Nest* (1951) with Jack Paar and Marilyn Monroe, and *The Girl Next Door* (1953).

In 1953, while making thirty-five hundred dollars a week, she announced she would not renew her Fox contract but that she would become a nun. When she entered the novitiate of the Sisters of Charity, at Xavier, Kansas, she was warned that she might be doing so to run away from life: a romance with composer David Rose in 1946 had come to nothing; she had been married to musician Jimmy Zito in 1947 and been divorced the following year; and in 1953 her fiancé, Dr. John Durzik, a dentist, had died of hemophilia. She left the convent after seven months.

In 1955 June married Fred MacMurray, for which she was deprived of the sacraments of her church since it did not recognize her divorce. Fred was forty-five, June was twenty-eight.

Subsequently, she did a Lux Radio Theatre show but was showing less and less interest in working. In 1958, after appearing with her husband on *The Lucille Ball–Desi Arnaz Show,* she announced her retirement.

She and MacMurray, one of the wealthiest stars in Hollywood, live on their ranch in the San Fernando Valley with their adopted twin daughters, Katie and Laurie. MacMurray's first wife by whom he had a daughter, now grown, is deceased. A contemporary of June's from her Fox days, Robert Arthur (now a partner in a Hollywood casting firm), who sees her now and then, says she has no desire to act again and has refused many parts, including guest spots on her husband's television shows.

With Jeanne Crain (left) at a recent opening. *Jon Virzi*

In the film *Wonder Bar*, 1934.

HAL LE ROY

The dancer-comedian was born in Cincinnati, Ohio, in 1913, the youngest of three boys, with the real name John Le Roy Schotte. When he was seven, his father, a lumber salesman, moved the family to Memphis, where Hal got a job selling newspapers. Two black newsboys, who customarily danced to amuse themselves and to attract customers, influenced Hal. He had been playing drums in the school band, and now he caught their sense of movement and he, too, began dancing on his street corner. Soon after, he was entertaining people aboard the Memphis riverboats, sometimes making as much as ten dollars in tips every ten miles or so. In 1925 the family returned to Cincinnati. Hal entered an amateur show and won a week's engagement at a theatre in nearby Covington, Kentucky. A well-known minstrel, Eddie Leonard, saw him work and suggested that he try his luck in New York. Mrs. Schotte took his advice and brought the fourteen-year-old boy to the Ned Wayburn Dancing School for his professional training and enrolled him at the Professional Children's School in New York where he completed two years of high school.

In 1928 Hal appeared at the Lyric Theatre in Hoboken, New Jersey, in a play called *Hoboken Hoboes* with Frank Tinney and Bert Fitzgibbons. From there he went into New York's Palace Theatre, the Paramount Grill, and the Central Park Casino. During his Casino engagement he received a note backstage requesting a meeting after the performance. It was signed "Flo Ziegfeld" but Hal thought it was a joke and disregarded it. When he found out later that the showman had been in the audience that night with Fred and Adele Astaire,* and had actually tried to see him, it was too late.

In 1930 he worked with songwriter Benny Davis in an act called "Future Stars of Broadway." Others in the show were Martha Raye, Buddy and Vilma Ebsen, and the late Jackie Heller. In 1931 their show played the Palace, and Hal was signed to do *The Gang's All Here,* a Broadway play which starred Ted Healy. During its run, Ziegfeld came backstage, and this time signed Hal for the *Follies*. Hal had been asking two hundred dollars per week but with Ziegfeld he got a bonus plus five hundred dollars a week. He appeared in the *Ziegfeld Follies of 1931,* which offered Jack Pearl * and Pearl's partner, Cliff Hall (who lives in Ridgefield, New Jersey), Gladys Glad (she is the widow of Mark Hellinger and lives in Manhattan), and the team of Buck and Bubbles (John Bubbles is retired in Los Angeles). Ziegfeld wanted to star Hal in a musical version of Booth Tarkington's *Seventeen,* but Ziegfeld died before his plans were completed.

Hal's biggest years were 1933 and 1934, when he was seen on Broadway in *Strike Me Pink* and *Thumbs Up* and at the Empire Room of the Waldorf Astoria, as well as in two Warner Bros. pictures: *Wonder Bar* with Al Jolson and the late Kay Francis and *Harold Teen* opposite Rochelle Hudson.

Some of Le Roy's other film credits are *Artists and Models* (1937) with Jack Benny and Gail Patrick (she quit acting to produce the *Perry Mason* television series and lives in Los Angeles) and *Blondie* (1938), which starred Penny Singleton ** and Arthur Lake.** Stage appearances followed in *Start Cheering* (1938), *Too Many Girls* (1938), and *Count Me In* (1942) with Mary Healy. His movie version of *Too Many Girls* was released in 1940, with chorus boy Van Johnson reenacting a Broadway role.

Hal was featured on Bob Hope's first television show, on Easter Sunday 1947, and has been seen on the *Ed Sullivan Show,* the *Dean Martin Show,* and *Hollywood Palace.*

But he returned to the footlights in 1956 in the role of Frank in Guy Lombardo's Jones Beach revival of *Show Boat.* In 1966 he was backstage again as director-choreographer of *Autumn's Here,* a musical version of *The Legend of Sleepy Hollow,* at the off-Broadway Bert Wheeler Theatre. Hal became more active behind the scenes during the sixties. He produced and directed industrial shows for Lytton Industries and Oldsmobile among others.

Hal is an active member of the Lambs' Club, and in 1968 produced and directed their famous *Lambs Gambol* show saluting Richard Rodgers, just as he had done for Milton Berle several years earlier. Hal and his wife of thirty-seven years, Ruth Dodd—one of twelve John Powers models who appeared with him in *Strike Me Pink*—have lived in Maywood, New Jersey, for thirty years. They have no children.

With author Lamparski's assistant Michael Knowles recently at the Lambs' Club, Manhattan. *Chris Albertson*

In the *Ziegfeld Follies of 1922.*

VIVIENNE SEGAL

The singing star of Broadway was born in Philadelphia in 1897. Her physician father was Dr. Bernard Segal. The exceptionally pretty Vivienne at an early age was enrolled with a singing coach. One day in 1915 Mrs. Segal, a very ambitious mother, learned that the Schuberts were having trouble finding a replacement for their leading lady in *The Blue Paradise*. Telling her husband that they had some local shopping to do, Mrs. Segal, with Vivienne, boarded a train for New York, where she managed an interview with J. J. Schubert and Sigmund Romberg, the producer and author. Both men agreed that Vivienne should be cast in the lead, despite her complete lack of experience on the Broadway stage. The play was a hit and Vivienne became a star. *The Blue Paradise* ran nearly a year.

In Jerome Kern and Victor Herbert's *Miss 1917* she headed a cast that included Marion Davies and Ann Pennington,** and in 1918 starred with Constance Binney (Mrs. C. B. Cheshire of Queens, New York, now raising pedigreed dogs) in *Oh! Lady, Lady!* She followed that with *The Little Whopper* (1919), was presented in the *Ziegfeld Follies of 1922* along with the late Gilda Gray, and in 1923 sang in the opera *Adrienne,* the year she married Robert Ames.

Undoubtedly, Vivienne's greatest triumph during her early career was her role in the original company of Sigmund Romberg's operetta *The Desert Song,* the smash hit of 1926. Like her debut, just before opening she had replaced the star originally slated for the part. Two years later Flo Ziegfeld starred her as Lady Constantine in his successful musical adaptation of *The Three Musketeers.*

When sound came to motion pictures, Warner Bros. gave her the opportunity to become a movie star, but *Viennese Nights* (1930), her first, with

Jean Hersholt, did not cause much of a stir. Two years later she made a Vitaphone short and then made *The Cat and the Fiddle* (1934) with Jeanette MacDonald and Ramon Novarro.* But she remained essentially a stage star. Vivienne lost nearly every cent she had when the stock market crashed in 1929. Her radio work during the thirties literally kept a roof over her head and enabled her to support her widowed mother, who lived with her.

Even though Vivienne was heard on radio during the thirties, when she opened in *I Married an Angel* in 1938, Broadway audiences saw her for the first time in eight years. Her exile had been self-imposed and her comeback vehicle was one of the season's hits. Also in the cast was the dazzling Vera Zorina.

Two years later Miss Segal topped her *Angel* success with the modern classic *Pal Joey*, in which her leading man was the young Gene Kelly, while buried in the chorus was an unknown Van Johnson. Twelve years later, *Joey* was as big a hit as ever in the Vivienne Segal–Harold Lang revival. Twenty-two years after movie audiences last saw her, Vivienne appeared in the June Allyson film *The Opposite Sex,* her last working appearance.

Vivienne's second husband was Hubbell Robinson, Jr., a former vice-president and production head of CBS Television, who, during his tenure with the network, made several announcements that his wife would be presented in a television series. Nothing ever came of it, though she did do a few guest shots in the early sixties on such programs as *Alfred Hitchcock Presents,* but by then Robinson was no longer with CBS. She and Robinson have been legally separated for a number of years but are still friendly. She lives alone on Sunset Plaza Drive, above Hollywood's Sunset Strip, only a few doors from her former rival and now long-time friend Peggy Fears. A serious heart condition rules out much social life or traveling for Vivienne, and working again is out of the question.

At home with her schnauzers. *Clifford May*

KING VIDOR

The director of some of Hollywood's finest films was born in Galveston, Texas, on February 8, 1894. He attended schools locally and spent his summers working around his father in lumber camps and sawmills until he was offered a job as a ticket-taker in a nickelodeon. During his twelve-hour day, for which he was paid $3.50 weekly, King also at times acted as the projectionist. He saw the 1907 version of *Ben Hur* 147 times.

While on vacation from Peacock Military Academy in San Antonio, King and a friend photographed a sixty-mile-per-hour windstorm, and he sold the film locally. After leaving school, he worked in Houston for a time with a newsreel company. Then he wrote a scenario called "In Tow," found a partner who owned a movie camera, and filmed it. He continued writing scenarios and completed fifty-two before he sold his first, *Southern Storm*. Altogether, he sold twenty but still could not meet his expenses.

The turning point in his life was in 1919. He married Florence Arlo from Houston and declared bankruptcy. However, the couple managed to buy a secondhand Model-T Ford and moved to Santa Monica, California. His wife began working at Vitagraph for ten dollars a week while King earned money as an extra. He then became a twelve-dollar-a-week clerk at Universal and soon made his first feature *The Turn in the Road* (1918), followed by a successful comedy-romance with Zasu Pitts called *Better Times* (1919).

Florence Vidor became a silent star with great appeal, whom he directed in *Dusk to Dawn* (1922). They were divorced in 1924. She later married violinist Jascha Heifetz and now lives in seclusion in Pacific Palisades, California. From 1926 to 1933 he was married to Eleanor Boardman, who was his star in *Three Wise Fools* (1923) and *Wine of Youth* (1924). At one point he kidnapped their two children from her, but the two have since become good friends and he visits her often in Santa Barbara.

King made over fifty more features, some of the most notable being *Peg O' My Heart* (1923), *Wife of the Centaur* (1925) with Aileen Pringle,** *Big Parade* (1925), *The Crowd* (1928), *Hallelujah* (1929), an Academy Award nomination, *The Champ* (1931), another nomination, *Street Scene* (1931), *Wedding Night* (1935) with Anna Sten,* *Stella Dallas* (1937), *Northwest Passage* (1940), *Duel in the Sun* (1946), *The Fountainhead* (1949), *Ruby Gentry* (1952), and *Man Without a Star* (1955). Vidor's last two films were his undoing: *War and Peace* (1956) and *Solomon and Sheba* (1959), which received very poor notices and lost staggering sums of money. Vidor had committed Hollywood's unpardonable sin—he was unsuccessful.

In 1953 his autobiography, *A Tree Is a Tree,* was published. During the sixties he taught a graduate class in cinema at UCLA. In 1964 Vidor's silent and sound pictures were honored with the Golden Thistle Award in Edinburgh, Scotland, at their film festival.

The director by no means considers himself retired and hopes to direct his completed screenplay about the life of Mary Baker Eddy. His name, however, does not impress the young men now running Hollywood. One recent letter of rejection was downright insulting.

Vidor's money was well invested, and he can afford to maintain a home in Beverly Hills, a ranch in San Luis Obispo, and a secretary.

Always a great ladies' man, lately he has been spending nearly all of his time in the company of the silent star Colleen Moore.**

The veteran Hollywood director today. *Gary Leavitt*

With the late Zasu Pitts (right) in *They Just Had to Get Married,* 1933.

FIFI D'ORSAY

The French Bombshell was born in Montreal, Canada, in 1904 with the name Yvonne Lussier. Her father, who had twelve other children, worked for thirty years in the local post office. Her first job was as a typist for six dollars a week, and this lasted a week, but she was hired immediately by another company for nine dollars a week. She had worked that up to thirty-five dollars a week by 1924, when she met George Edwards, a New York producer, who gave her the usual line to look him up if she ever came to New York. Two family friends financed her trip. The late Helen Morgan, whom she met during a personal appearance in Montreal, greeted her at the station in New York. Fifi made the rounds, and within six months she was in the chorus of *Greenwich Village Follies.* While touring with the show in 1925, the comedy team Gallagher and Sheen took an interest in her and worked her into their famous act. Fifi went over so well that they used her again, in *In Dutch,* which had a very short run in 1926.

She worked steadily in vaudeville from 1926 to 1929 in an act called "Ten Dollars a Lesson." She impressed Will Rogers, who asked Fox to test her for *They Had to See Paris* (1929). The film and Fifi were great hits. Sound was in, and she had a cute, sexy French accent. The studio had great plans for her. She made *Just Imagine* (1930), *The Girl from Calgary* (1932) with the late Paul Kelly and Astrid Allwyn (now Mrs. Charles Fee of Beverly Hills), *Going Hollywood* (1933) in which Bing Crosby crooned the hit song "Temptation," and *Accent on Youth* (1935) with the late Herbert Marshall.

When Fifi learned that Fox, paying her four hundred dollars a week, made huge amounts of money when she was loaned out to other studios, she was irked. She left Fox, ignoring her seven-year contract.

Fifi had played presentation houses and knew the kind of receipts movie stars could draw in such personal appearances, as in 1932 when she, the late Victor McLaglin, and Edmund Lowe headlined the bill at New York's Capitol, and set records. She went out on her own, and her first booking was for five thousand dollars a week. But what Fifi didn't seem to realize was that she was a big name because she was a movie star, and that she could only remain so by making movies. Breaking her Fox contract closed nearly every Hollywood door to her.

By the forties, Fifi, whose trademark was "Ello, beeg boy!" had been working in cheap movies and radio for a number of years, but her heyday was definitely over. She had no funds to fall back on; in the days when she was making five thousand dollars a week she was spending six thousand, supporting not only her family but moving about with a large entourage. "I had a very good time," she said, "and I had a lot of people around me who were having a good time."

She attempted a comeback at the Palace Theatre in 1950 when eighteen months earlier she could not have been booked into a benefit, according to her. (Three thousand appearances entertaining United States troops had not seemed to arouse any GI interest in paying to see her.) In 1952 Ralph Edwards saluted her on his *This Is Your Life* television show, which she hoped would reactivate her career, but nothing much happened except she cashed in her gift of a round-trip plane ticket to Paris. Fifi has since appeared on television talk shows such as the Joey Bishop show and has done small parts in the films *Wild and Wonderful* (1964) and *The Art of Love* (1965), among others.

She has been married twice but has been single for a number of years. She lives alone in a small Hollywood apartment and is a daily communicant at a local Roman Catholic church. When recognized, it is as much for her voice as her appearance—she still has that distinctive, heavy French accent, even though she has never set foot outside North America. She has become an excellent lecturer on a subject she calls "I'm Glad I'm Not Young Anymore." If she could relive her life, she says she would "make some mistakes more often and sooner." When last heard from, Fifi hoped to make an adult Western in which "I would kees the horse and jump on the cowboy."

The French Bombshell in a recent interview with the author. *Clifford May*

Made up for a publicity picture, 1947.
NBC Radio

"JUST PLAIN BILL": Arthur Hughes

One of the earliest and most durable of all soap operas, *Just Plain Bill,* went on the air in September 1932. The title role was played by Arthur Hughes, a character actor who had already distinguished himself on Broadway in such plays *Mourning Becomes Electra* and *Elizabeth the Queen.*

The character Just Plain Bill was completely without pretension. To the folks who lived in the mythical town of Hartville, Bill Davidson was a man they could go to in time of trouble knowing he would give them sound advice and any personal help within his power. Because the setting was a small country town, *Just Plain Bill* probably lacked some of the drama and absurd situations that kept popping up on most other daytime serials, but the character of Bill was a strong one, and the program lasted until 1955. For most of its years, the series was heard in the late afternoons, five days a week, over NBC Radio. It was sandwiched in with *Stella Dallas, Portia Faces Life,* and *Lorenzo Jones.*

Bill was the town barber and listened all day to local gossip and people's troubles. He never butted in where he was not invited, and remained philosophical about his own woes. He was a widower, and his only child, Nancy (played by Ruth Russell, still an actress and in touch with Hughes), had married wealthy and socially prominent Kerry Donovan (played by James Meighan, a Long Island resident now). The show's announcers were Andre Baruch and Ed Herlihy.

Although there was never any favoritism shown, most actors of the day felt that *Just Plain Bill,* one of several Hummert productions, was the Hummerts' personal favorite. (Frank Hummert is dead; Anne Hummert lives alone in Manhattan and keeps in touch with Mr. and Mrs. Hughes.) One regular on the show was Teri Keane (still living in Manhattan and acting on television), who played the part of Dorothy Nash, as well as the title character on another radio show, *The Second Mrs. Burton,* and the part of Chi-Chi on *Life Can Be Beautiful. Just Plain Bill*'s Jonathan Hillery was performed by relatively unknown MacDonald Carey. A distinctive feature of the series was its two musical themes: Hal Brown strummed "Darling Nelly Gray" on guitar at the opening and "Polly Wolly Doodle" on his harmonica at the close.

Unlike most performers who starred in soap operas, Arthur Hughes is very much like the character he portrayed: a serious, thoughtful man of the "old school," and today, at over seventy, is considerably more like Bill than when he performed.

Arthur has been married since 1933 to former actress Geneva Harrison, seen many years ago on Broadway with the Lunts in such plays as *The Guardsman* (1924) and *Caprice* (1928). The Hugheses have no children and live quietly on West End Avenue in Manhattan. Because of his easily recognizable voice, neighbors still refer to him as Bill. Contemporaries of radio's golden age always considered Arthur an actor's actor: before each program he would go off in a corner with the script, his lines marked in red pencil, and practically memorize them; it did not matter that the show had already been rehearsed. He earned his colleagues' highest compliment: "very professional."

Few who saw the hit musical *How Now Dow-Jones?* (1968) recognized the kindly barber from Hartville in the role of the eccentric millionaire who brought down the house with the line "Tough titty." One matron, though, noticed his credits in the playbill: "I never peel potatoes for dinner that I don't miss that program."

During a recent interview at WBAI–FM in New York City. *Clifford May*

With sister Rosetta (left) and daughter Evalyn, 1933. *UPI*

VIVIAN DUNCAN

The surviving member of the world-famous Duncan sisters was born in Los Angeles, California, in 1899, two years before her sister Rosetta. Mother Duncan died when they were very young. Mr. Duncan divided his time between being a violinist and a real estate salesman.

In 1911, while the girls were playing amateur nights, their older sister, Evelyn, who was in the Broadway show *Fair and Warmer,* took them to the famous Gus Edwards. Lila Lee * and Georgie Price were leaving Edwards's cast of *The Kiddies' Revue.* The Duncan sisters replaced them. Vivian was the prettier of the two but Rosetta was the better performer. They took singing lessons as a gift from Nora Bayes, a headliner of the day, and they wrote much of their own music, arrangements, and dialogue.

Ziegfeld saw them touring in San Francisco and put them into *Doing Our Bit* in 1917, followed by *She's a Good Fellow* in 1919 and *Tip-Top* in 1921.

The girls' smash hit was their own creation. As *Topsy and Eva* they opened in San Francisco in 1923, with Rosetta playing Topsy in blackface. It ran sixteen weeks and moved to Los Angeles. When it opened on Broadway in 1924, the sisters became the toasts of New York. A Chicago engagement lasted a full year. As they toured England, the Continent, and South Africa in their production, Vivian and Rosetta were wined and dined by King George of Greece, Emanuel of Portugal, the Duke of Windsor, and Alfonso of Spain.

No personalities typified the glamour of American show people more than the Duncan sisters during the Roaring Twenties. They made the 1927 silent-film version of *Topsy and Eva*—a failure—and *It's a Great Life* (1929). Walter Winchell paid them one thousand dollars a minute to sing on his radio show.

In the 1929 crash, the Duncans lost over a million dollars, but it didn't slow them down. They worked in vaudeville and opened a drama school in Burlingame. The team worked occasionally in presentation houses and on radio until the forties, when they announced their retirement.

In 1952 they started all over again with television appearances and club dates in which they performed the songs they made famous: "Rememb'ring," "Bye, Bye, Blackbird," and "Side by Side." In 1957 they headlined the show for the fifty-first anniversary of the Palace Theatre.

In 1959, while playing a club date in the Midwest, Rosetta was killed in a car accident. Four months later Vivian began her act as a single and hasn't stopped since. "I'll never retire," she said recently. "As long as I spend all my time at the piano I may as well make some money at the same time." In 1968 she toured clubs in Australia for a year.

Evelyn Duncan lives in Los Angeles and has two children. Brother Harold is a former tennis champion and songwriter. Vivian lives with her husband, retired builder Frank Herman, on a two-acre estate in Atherton, California. They have been married since 1947. She has a daughter by her first husband, Nils Asther (acting with the Royal Theatre in Copenhagen) whom she divorced in 1932. Evelyn makes frequent visits to Los Angeles, where she sees such old friends as Penny Singleton ** and Rose Perfect (retired and living in Los Angeles).

During a recent trip to Hollywood. *Clifford May*

On a Bermuda vacation, 1931. *UPI*

RUDOLPH FRIML

The schmaltz king of music was born in Prague, Bohemia (Czechoslovakia), in 1879. When he was little more than a baby, his mother insisted he learn to play the piano, and by six he was playing professionally. At ten he composed a barcarolle and four years later was enrolled in the Prague Conservatory of Music, where he spent three years studying composition under Anton Dvořák. His piano teacher had been Jiranek. After graduation he and a fellow student, violinist Jan Kubelik, toured Europe, and ended in a 1901 concert in the United States. In 1904 Friml performed his own composition, Piano Concerto in B-Major, in Carnegie Hall with Walter Damrosch conducting the New York Symphony, and from 1906 to 1912 he appeared as piano virtuoso with the Boston and Philadelphia symphonies.

Friml's first chance to compose for musical comedy came when Victor Herbert, during a performance of *Naughty Marietta,* fought with the star, Emma Trentini. Herbert and Trentini had already been signed to do the new Arthur Hammerstein show, *The Firefly* (1912). Friml, although he seemed poorly equipped to write for operettas, replaced him. The association worked out so well that when Friml's wife divorced him in 1915 she named Miss Trentini as corespondent. Friml wrote *Firefly* in one month. It was a smash hit and contained such gems as "Giannina Mia," and the waltz "Sympathy" (later rewritten as "The Donkey Serenade").

From then on until his last hit, *The Three Musketeers* (1928), Friml was one of the two top composers on Broadway, his only rival being Sigmund Romberg. However, Friml won fame more quickly and easily, and had more hits. Some of his shows that lit up Broadway marquees were *Kitty Darlin'* (1917), *Sometime* (1918) which starred Ed Wynn, Mae West, and Francine Larrimore (retired and alternating between New York and Vermont), *High*

Jinks (1914), *Katinka* (1915) with Herbert Stothart, *Rose-Marie* (1924), and *The Vagabond King* (1925). The last two ran five hundred performances each, incredible for the time, with *Rose-Marie* being done in three different films and *The Vagabond King* in two. His nineteen-year-old granddaughter, Dian had a small part in the last *Vagabond* version, in 1955.

For the last forty years, Friml has lived quietly in the Hollywood hills. Everyone who meets Friml is amazed at his endless vitality. His other most noticeable quality is his concern for money. In spite of his age and wealth he has been known to accept passage on a transoceanic steamship in exchange for services at the piano en route. Since 1952 Friml has been married to his fourth wife, the former Mary Ling, who had been his secretary for fourteen years before they wed. Mrs. Friml, an American-born Chinese, is twenty-five years his junior.

Although it is a long time since he has been produced, the nonagenarian still writes melodies, which he records with himself at the piano. His only comment on the music of today is his walking out of a performance of *My Fair Lady,* complaining that "nobody sings." He says that he tries to avoid hearing today's composers so he cannot even unconsciously copy them. He firmly believes that his kind of music will again be appreciated, and not only by those who subscribe to Muzak, the source of much of his income now.

Friml's last publicized public appearance was in New York in December 1969, when the American Society of Composers, Authors, and Publishers, (founded in 1914) of which he is a charter member, gave him a ninetieth-birthday party at the Shubert Theatre. The composer of thirty-three operettas was onstage most of the evening, talking with the audience, playing his own compositions, and doing little dances that were not part of the program. The *New York Times* described it as "an orgy of schmaltz."

Friml is currently working on a new musical, *Castle in Spain,* and is considering another with an oriental motif.

The nonagenarian on his last birthday.
Beltz

Under contract to Paramount, 1942.

SUSANNA FOSTER

Suzanne DeLee Flanders Larson was the movie songstress's real name. She was born in Chicago in 1924 and reared in Minneapolis, Minnesota. When she was eleven years old, some unremembered persons had recorded her voice and sent the record to Metro-Goldwyn-Mayer. The studio had only recently let Deanna Durbin out of her contract, whereupon she had gone straight to Universal and rescued them from bankruptcy by her popularity. M-G-M was therefore quite receptive to having under contract a pretty little girl so young and talented. She wasn't as cute as their Judy Garland or as pretty as Deanna Durbin, but her voice was phenomenal, and it was the era of child stars. Susanna was promptly given a voice coach, which—according to Susanna, who had never taken lessons—nearly ruined her voice. After a year she was called into Nicholas Nafack's office and told that she was not a singer, but might have some acting ability. Nafack was the brother-in-law of Eddie Mannix, one of the studio heads, and married to a girl who considered herself a singer. Susanna's option was dropped.

Paramount auditioned her for a walk-on in *The Great Victor Herbert* (1939) and so impressed director Le Roy Prinz that he got her a big part in the movie. She was placed under contract and did three more pictures: *Glamour Boy* (1941) with Jackie Cooper (until recently vice-president in charge of production for Screen Gems, Columbia Pictures' television subsidiary), *The Hard-Boiled Canary* (1941), and *Star Spangled Rhythm* (1942). When her option was up for renewal they offered to continue her contract without her entitled raise. Susanna, who was her own manager, turned them down flat, and, with no other offers or prospects, left the lot.

Forty days later she signed with Universal for her best part: she played opposite the late Nelson Eddy and Claude Rains in *The Phantom of the Opera* (1943). Actually, Susanna was brought to the Valley lot to act as a threat to Deanna Durbin, and it was to Miss Durbin that all the plum parts went. Susanna at first was unaware of the plot. In fact, she was an avid Durbin fan. Other films followed: *Follow the Boys* (1944), *This Is the Life* (1944), *The Climax* (1944) with the late Boris Karloff, *Bowery to Broadway* (1944), *Frisco Sal* (1945) with Turhan Bey (now a commercial photographer in Vienna, Austria), and *That Night With You* (1945) opposite the late Franchot Tone.

When option time came around she informed the front office that she was retiring. Susanna knew that they simply could not give her the vehicles suited to her talents and that she would continue in one mediocre film after another. The best they could offer was the lead in *The Countess of Monte Cristo* made by Sonja Henie * in 1948.

She says of rumors that she wanted to go into opera: "I knew enough about opera to know that the politics were even worse than in the studio. I was never really ambitious. At least not in the cutthroat way that's required to succeed. The truth is that I hated a career and everything that went with it."

In 1948 she married Wilbur Evans, a singer. The marriage lasted twelve years and produced two sons, Michael and Philip. The divorce was quite bitter, with considerable litigation concerning child support. In the single interview she has given in a decade, Susanna asked her radio audience the whereabouts of her ex-husband (knowledgeable listeners were to get in touch with her or her lawyer so they could serve him with papers) and for a part-time job to help support her teen-age boys (she works during the day at Merrill, Lynch, Pierce, Fenner & Smith's Wall Street office, in the dividend department, but seeks a night job also in order to keep her sons in private school). The older boy is part of a rock group called the Sugar Blues Band.

Susanna Foster's autograph is one of the most sought-after among collectors, and her fans all over the world outnumber those of many former top stars. She has been offered parts in off-Broadway plays, television shows, and nightclub tours, but steadfastly refuses every one. "I want to do what I want to do and that does not include anything in show business," was her final comment about her unusual career.

Entertaining recently in her West Side Manhattan apartment. *Courtney Wright*

In *The Woman I Love,* 1937.

STERLING HOLLOWAY

The professional bumpkin was born in 1905 in Cedartown, Georgia. He came to New York while still in his teens and studied at Sargent's Dramatic School. While learning his craft, Sterling was able to pick up a little money in walk-on parts of Theatre Guild productions.

In 1925, when the Lunt-Fontanne production of *The Guardsman* was playing at the Garrick Theatre, Sterling, who with some other young artists had put together burlesques of plays that were currently big hits on Broadway, helped put together one for the Garrick on Sundays, when the theatre would ordinarily be dark. *Garrick Gaieties* was such a success that when it opened it took over the theatre completely and ran through four editions. Holloway was in the 1925 and 1926 versions along with newcomers Romney Brent (residing in Mexico City) and Sanford Meisner and Lee Strasberg (now two of the most important drama coaches in the country). Richard Rodgers conducted the orchestra, which played his and Lorenz Hart's songs. Holloway introduced the hit songs of the shows: "Manhattan" in 1925 and "Mountain Greenery" in 1926.

He went to Hollywood, where he made two-reelers and the Wallace Beery feature *Casey at the Bat,* but he disliked the silent film so much that he returned to New York, convinced that he should forget about movies. One director agreed, telling Sterling that his hillbilly features were "too repulsive." But after stints in vaudeville and a couple more plays, he returned to Hollywood and worked constantly throughout the thirties and into the forties.

Among the over one hundred films he appeared in were *Alice in Wonderland* (1933), *Elmer the Great* (1933) with Joe E. Brown,** *Life Begins at 40* (1935) with Will Rogers, *Rendezvous* (1935) with William Powell,** *Palm Springs* (1936) with Frances Langford,** *Career Woman* (1936) with Michael Whalen (retired and living in Encino, California), *The Bluebird* (1940), *A Walk in the Sun* (1945), *The Beautiful Blonde from Bashful Bend* (1949), and *Shake, Rattle and Rock* (1956).

164

Holloway appeared less and less in films as he began to resist the type-casting Hollywood imposed on him. He told an interviewer, "I delivered so many telegrams and jerked so many sodas I got tired of it." He demanded meatier parts, and when they did not come, he returned to the stage, working at the Pasadena Playhouse and the Los Angeles Civic Light Opera. As well as acting and singing, he directed a number of the productions. Since 1956 Sterling has done summer stock in Sacramento, California, every season. He is seen nearly every year in several productions at the Theatre in the Round in Seattle, Washington. His last motion picture was *Live a Little, Love a Little* (1968) with Elvis Presley.

From 1953 to 1958 Sterling played the part of Waldo on the William Bendix series *The Life of Riley*. During the 1964–1965 season Holloway played a running part on the television series *The Baileys of Balboa*. Sterling's voice backed many of Walt Disney's animals, both in nature films and cartoons. The children's records he did for Disney have sold steadily year after year, providing him with a substantial income.

Sterling lives in a hilltop house in South Laguna, California. He has never married because he does not feel lacking in anything and doesn't wish to disturb his pattern of life. Some years ago he began to collect paintings and now has a collection valued at over seven hundred and fifty thousand dollars. Many of the paintings by artists such as Roy Lichtenstein were bought before they had become fashionable—and expensive.

About his career, Holloway says that he is ready and willing for parts in feature films but insists that he can do and has done more than comedy. While he doesn't mind being thought of as a comedian, he wants to avoid playing the yokel again and again.

Very much at home in California.

A Paramount still, 1935.

EVELYN VENABLE

The demure beauty of the silver screen in the 1930s was born in 1913 in Cincinnati, Ohio. Her father and grandfather were writers and teachers. Evelyn attended Walnut Hills High School in Cincinnati, where it had been an annual tradition for the drama department to present a Shakespearean play under almost professional conditions. She played Juliet one year and Rosalind in *As You Like It* the next. Her performances were so impressive for a girl with very little training that she won a part in a professional production of *Dear Brutus,* presented at the local Civic Center.

The summer after she graduated, her father took her to the home of his friend actor-director Walter Hampden, who asked her to read Juliet to his Romeo. Impressed with the sixteen-year-old, Hampden told the Venables that although she had talent he could not engage her at that time but would send for her if a place became available in his stock company.

Evelyn thereafter won a four-year scholarship to Vassar, but left at the end of her freshman year to continue her studies at the University of Cincinnati. She did not take drama at either institution.

In 1932 to 1933 she toured with Hampden's company, playing Ophelia to his Hamlet, and in *Cyrano de Bergerac.* A talent scout for Paramount Pictures caught her Ophelia at the Biltmore Theatre in Los Angeles. Offered a contract, Evelyn had strong misgivings about leaving the Hampden company, but the studio told her that she would be put into *Cradle Song* (1933) with Dorothea Wieck (living in West Berlin). She went with Paramount, where at first her roles were good. She made *Mrs. Wiggs of the Cabbage Patch* (1934) with Pauline Lord, W. C. Fields, and Edith Fellowes (married and living in Manhattan), *Death Takes a Holiday* (1934), *David Harum* (1934) with Will Rogers and Stepin Fetchit,* and *Alice Adams* (1935), but after those it was downhill all the way. There were pictures such as a *Cisco Kid* episode, *The Frontiersman* (1938) with William Boyd ** and *The*

166

Headleys at Home (1938). She took some time off to bear two daughters, and upon her return was given a role opposite the late Stu Erwin in *He Hired the Boss* (1943). Evelyn simply did not have the interest to continue and announced her retirement.

In a recent interview she explained: "I'd seen so many Hollywood families come apart because of the mother's career. I wanted to be with the girls when they began to ask important questions. During the war I worked a great deal for the Red Cross. I've never regretted leaving films. If I have any regrets at all it is in leaving the stage. I might have been a really good actress. There simply was no chance in most of my pictures nor was I getting the proper training after I left Mr. Hampden."

While at Paramount she was promoted for a time as "the kissless girl," a title she still does not understand. "Even my dad, who was rather strict with me, thought it was ridiculous. I never lacked for kisses either in or out of pictures."

After twenty-five years away from college, Evelyn registered at UCLA, where she studied Greek and Latin. When she received her degree, the department head startled her by asking if she would like to stay as an instructor. She has been a faculty member ever since. "Once in a while," she says, "a student from the cinema department will drop by my office after class and ask me about the old days, but very few of my students know that I was in movies and the ones that do, don't care. I'm just their teacher and friend and I love it."

For over thirty years Evelyn has been married to cameraman Hal Mohr. A few years ago, after their daughters had left home, they moved into a charming cottage in the Brentwood section of Los Angeles along with their several cats and Mohr's Oscar for cinematography in *Midsummer Night's Dream* (1935).

The Mohrs eat "no organism with conscious life." Mohr has been a vegetarian since their marriage, but Evelyn has never tasted meat or fish in her life. One of the Mohrs' friends from show business is Norman Frescott, who for years was the vaudeville headliner "The Great Frescott," a top mind-reading act of the day.

At home in Brentwood. *Clifford May*

In Washington, D.C., 1943. *UPI*

JERRY VOORHIS

The congressman stepping-stone for Richard M. Nixon's political career was born in Ottawa, Kansas, in 1901. He attended schools in Michigan, Illinois, Missouri, Oklahoma, Colorado, and Connecticut, receiving a B.A., with Phi Beta Kappa standing, from Yale in 1923. Jerry went to work in a factory for thirty-nine cents an hour and in 1924 he traveled to Germany on a good-will tour for the Young Men's Christian Association. Later he worked in a freight yard and on a farm before becoming a schoolteacher at the Allendale Farm School in Illinois. In Wyoming he opened the first home for orphan boys. He received a master's degree in education from Clarement College, California, where from 1928 to 1938 he conducted the Voorhis School for Boys.

Voorhis was a Socialist until the advent of the New Deal, which he embraced enthusiastically, announcing that FDR's plans, if put into law, would make socialism unnecessary. Although his father was wealthy, Voorhis was always a liberal in matters of economics.

In 1934 he made an unsuccessful run for the California Senate, but in 1936 he was elected to the House of Representatives from the Twelfth District as a Democrat. For the first three years he was a bitter critic of the Dies Committee (officially the House Un-American Activities Committee) but in 1939 he was appointed to it and served under its chairman, Martin Dies.* His presence on the committee is generally considered the chief reason for its far more temperate reports than in the years before.

Although Nixon would make much of Voorhis's early days as a Socialist, the congressman was hardly the radical Left's favorite since he authored the Voorhis Act of 1940. That act required the registration of all agencies and

168

organizations with foreign affiliations. The United States Communist party was so troubled by the law that they held a special convention in New York only a month after FDR signed it to "cancel and dissolve its organizational affiliation to the Communist International."

After five terms in the House as a Democratic liberal, Voorhis was challenged for his seat by a young Republican former naval officer named Richard Milhous Nixon. In California, when candidates filed in both party primaries, Voorhis won not only the Democratic nomination but captured a large minority of Republican votes. But in the subsequent election campaign, Nixon's tactics—which he used a few years later when he unseated Senator Helen Gahagan Douglas—were to keep his opponent on the defensive, and Voorhis found himself defending insinuations and misrepresentations throughout most of the campaign. One Nixon newspaper ad read: "A vote for Nixon is a vote against the Communist-dominated Political Action Committee gigantic slush fund." And there were cries about "lip-service Americans" and officials "fronting for un-American elements" by "seeking increasing federal controls over the lives of the people." Just before the election, the Nixon forces released a paper that cried out against "the insolence of Moscow in telling the American voter to elect PAC candidates such as Voorhis."

With the district ruthlessly gerrymandered by a GOP legislature a few years before, the 1946 election was a landslide for the Republicans. But despite Nixon's win, which was assured without the vile tactics, his record in this race has been an embarrassment to him ever since.

Jerry Voorhis moved almost immediately to Winnetka, Illinois, with his family, and became executive director of the Cooperative League of the United States. He is now retired, but remains a strong proponent of cooperatives and is active in social and church work.

Shortly after Nixon's presidential election, Voorhis, asked how he felt, replied: "The one thing I do not want to do is comment on Mr. Nixon."

The former congressman photographed recently in Winnetka, Illinois. *Diana Keyt*

The bird-brained blond, 1941.

JOYCE COMPTON

Hollywood's favorite dumb blond was born in Lexington, Kentucky. Her parents traveled a great deal, consequently Joyce was schooled in Texas, Kansas, Canada, and Oklahoma. She entered films in 1925 as a result of a beauty contest. Her first part was in *Ankles Preferred* (1925), and this was followed by *What Fools Men* (1925).

In 1926 Joyce was chosen to be a Wampus Baby Star. Among twelve others who were chosen were Dolores Costello,** Janet Gaynor,** Fay Wray,** and Joan Crawford.

Joyce fared much better in talkies, where her southern drawl was used to advantage in one dizzy role after another. She started in 1929 with two Clara Bow vehicles, *Wild Party* and *Dangerous Curves,* and was with George O'Brien in *Salute.* Mack Sennett hired her in 1933 for a series of two-reel comedies, in which she costarred with Walter Catlett, Franklin Pangborn, and Grady Sutton. She found the work tiring and the atmosphere "haphazard." Although her Sennett period established her as a comedienne, it was the costar who usually got the laughs. Mainly, she was a foil for such comics as Clark & McCullough or Charlie Chase. Among the over two hundred features she appeared in were *Only Yesterday* (1933) with the late Billie Burke, *Sing, Sinner, Sing* (1943) with Leila Hyams (now Mrs. Phil Berg of

Bel Air, California), *Magnificent Obsession* (1935), *Love Before Breakfast* (1936) with the late Preston Foster, *The Awful Truth* (1937), with Irene Dunne,** *They Drive by Night* (1940), *Manpower* (1941), *Mildred Pierce* (1945), *Danger Signal* (1945) with Faye Emerson,** *Night and Day* (1946), *Sorry, Wrong Number* (1948), and Mighty Joe Young (1949).

After the death of her mother, in 1953, Joyce spent most of her time with her father. He died in 1965, leaving Joyce without any close relatives. In 1957, she appeared in *Jet Pilot,* made several years earlier. Her only television appearance was on *Pete and Gladys* in 1961.

Today Joyce lives with another family in the large Tudor house in Sherman Oaks, California, that she designed, with her parents' help. Begun in 1935, it was a long time in the building process, because whenever Joyce was laid off from film work, construction had to stop. She devotes many hours to part-time nursing and church work and, for years now, to her painting. She feels just about ready for a one-woman show.

Joyce often is recognized by fans but they are hesitant to mention that they remember her best as a dumb blond. When film historian Leonard Maltin asked her about the way she was typecast in Hollywood, she replied: "Sometimes one has to be smart to play dumb!"

At home in Sherman Oaks.

Beefcake, 1940.

JON HALL

Mrs. Locher's train was stopped in Fresno, California, in 1913, to allow Charles Hall Locher (his real name) to be born moments later. Jon's maternal grandmother had been queen of Tahiti, and his father a figure-skating champion in 1910 and 1911. Jon studied engineering, languages, and the sciences in England and Switzerland.

Jon says that he had no interest in acting until Sam Goldwyn noticed him sitting in the office of a producer. Jon was waiting for his uncle, writer Norman Hall, coauthor with Charles Nordhoff of *Mutiny on the Bounty* and *Hurricane*. Goldwyn offered him a contract for five hundred dollars a week. Jon signed it and was overnight a star via his role in *The Hurricane* (1937) with Mary Astor (residing in Mexico) and Dorothy Lamour. So much for the story Jon Hall likes to give interviewers. Now for the truth: Jon made at least five pictures in 1935 and 1936 under the name Charles Locher; he even had a contract with Twentieth Century-Fox under that name. One of those films was *Charlie Chan in Shanghai* (1935). Under another name, Lloyd Crane, he made *Mind Your Own Business* (1936) and *The Girl from Scotland Yard* (1937) with Karen Morley (the blacklisted actress lives in Los Angeles).

After *Hurricane* he was a hot property and was billed as "Goldwyn's Gift to Women." Because he had swum well since his fifth birthday, he was able to do his own water stunts, including a 131-foot dive. His young-man-in-a-loincloth image held on, despite quite a few Westerns to his credit. Some of those South Seas films are *Aloma of the South Seas* (1941), *On the Isle of Samoa* (1950), and *Forbidden Island* (1959). His other specialty was exotic locales: *Arabian Nights* (1942), *Ali Baba and the Forty Thieves* (1944),

Lady in the Dark (1944), *Cobra Woman* (1944) with the late Maria Montez and Sabu, *Sudan* (1945), and *Zamba* (1949). Aside from *Hurricane, Lady* is his only picture taken seriously today. The rest were matinee fare, particularly *When the Redskins Rode* (1951), *Brave Warrior* (1952), and *Beach Girls and the Monster* (1965).

Beginning in 1953, Hall made a great deal of money on his *Romar of the Jungle* television series, syndicated nationally for several years; he had a piece of the action, and it still plays in various parts of the world.

The heartthrob of the forties lives in the Los Feliz section of Los Angeles with his psychiatrist wife and her two sons and daughter. They were married in 1969 after Jon's divorce from Racquel Ames, his wife since 1959, who was preceded by Frances Langford ** for seventeen years.

Jon hasn't seen or heard from Dorothy Lamour in nearly a decade and sees few friends in the motion picture business on a social level. However, he is still very involved in movies: he is the producer of *The Side-Hackers* (1969), a low-budget motorcycle film, and the owner of some of the finest camera equipment in Hollywood; his cameras won an Oscar for cinematography (*Who's Afraid of Virginia Woolf*) in 1966. Even before he retired from acting, Hall owned and managed companies that built boats and underwater-camera housing for the navy, and he operated a fleet of airplanes and a flying school. He owns the copyright on Fantascope, a lens that can be adapted to any camera to provide a wider view of a subject, similar to the wide-screen processes in motion picturs. He operates from a large building in West Los Angeles that houses the Jon Hall Industries.

He told an interviewer recently: "I never liked acting. I don't like to be told what to do and what to say and how to say it. I'm grateful to it as it provided me with the money to do other things such as I'm into now, but as a profession, it's a bore."

At his West Los Angeles office today. *Dick Lynch*

At the crossroads between the silents and the talkies.

MAY McAVOY

The leading lady of silents and of the first talking picture was born in the family brownstone at Forty-first Street and Park Avenue in Manhattan in 1901. Her father and paternal grandfather owned and operated a huge livery stable that filled the block now occupied by the Waldorf-Astoria Hotel. "I wanted to be somebody," said May, and she tried to get her mother to allow her to become an actress. Even after an agent approached her, Mrs. McAvoy was against the idea. She was set on May becoming a schoolteacher. But when Mrs. McAvoy realized how unhappy her daughter would be if deprived of her chance, she relented.

Armed with photos of herself, May visited the various casting offices around New York, and found them very receptive. Her first job was for a commercial for Domino Sugar, which led to modeling jobs, and to movies. She looked even younger than she was, and she is short (reassuring to male leads), features then much sought after in actresses. From an extra role in *I'll Say So* (1918) she won a role in *Hate* (1917), filmed in Savannah, Georgia. Her notices were so good that she was hired for *To Hell with the Kaiser* (1918). Then for a couple of years she was an ingenue in vehicles for such top stars as the late Norma Talmadge and Florence Reed until studio executive J. Stuart Blackton made her a leading lady at Pathé. She wanted very badly to play the lead in *Sentimental Tommy* by Sir James Barrie, but the part had been cast. However, the star Faire Binney proved inadequate, and May, who had impressed the director with her work in *The Devil's Garden* (1920), replaced her. The film was released in 1921 and made stars of May and the late Gareth Hughes.

When May arrived in Hollywood at age twenty years she was already a star, but knew practically no one. Paramount had signed her to a contract and she was at once put to work in one programmer after another. She had such directors as William C. De Mille, John Robertson, George Fitzmaurice, and William Desmond Taylor, whose sensational murder in 1922 has never been solved. Cecil B. De Mille wanted her for a part in one of his epics, but when told that she would be nearly nude, she refused. He never spoke to her again. May was doing very well at Paramount and had her heart set on appearing in *The Little Minister* or *Peter Pan*. But she lost out on both, subsequently buying out her contract. However, she returned on a free-lance basis, though at fifteen hundred dollars—three times her previous salary. She appeared in *The Enchanted Cottage* (1924), making a great hit, and did *Lady Windermere's Fan* (1925), for which she got three thousand dollars a week.

May replaced Gertrude Olmstead (now retired in Los Angeles) in *Ben Hur* (1926) in the role of Esther. It seemed an endless role because the Italian extras and workmen who never had it so good did not want the production ever to end, and they continuously sabotaged the sets. There were even threats to kidnap May. One day, when she was talking to F. Scott Fitzgerald, a set exploded in flames right in front of them.

In 1927 May signed a contract with Warner Bros. She was given the part opposite Al Jolson in the first picture ever to have dialogue and music. May considered it little more than a novelty. The movie was *The Jazz Singer* (1927). It is ironic that May McAvoy should have starred in a production that ended both the silent era and her career. But her career ended not for the reason usually thought, that she had a lisp, but because she retired to marry G. Cleary, then vice-president and treasurer of United Artists. Before the marriage in 1929, she had the distinction of starring in England's first talkie, *The Terror* (1928), as well as adding several talkies to her career.

From 1940 until the midfifties May McAvoy was under contract to M-G-M, for which she made countless appearances in bit roles. She was unbilled and mostly unnoticed by fans who had known her as a star. One of her few friends from the old days is Viola Dana (unmarried and living alone in Santa Monica).

Her husband, who has been in poor health, retired after thirty years with Lockheed Aircraft. Their only child, Patrick, is married and has three children. The Clearys live just off Wilshire Boulevard in Beverly Hills in a small house furnished with what could be pieces from one of her old movie sets.

In the den of her Beverly Hills home.
Michael Knowles

In 1940 when he appeared in five films.

OTTO KRUGER

The leading man and character actor was born in Toledo, Ohio, in 1885. His stage debut came at age fifteen, when he played a small part in a production of *Quo Vadis?* in Toledo. Between seasons with stock and repertory companies, he managed to study for several semesters at both the University of Michigan and Columbia University.

He debuted on Broadway in *The Natural Law* in 1915, followed by *Young America* the same year and, *Captain Kidd, Jr.* in 1916.

In 1918 Kruger asked Peggy Wood to be his wife. She declined, saying she didn't believe in marriage. He admits now with some amusement that he was rather shocked at her proposal that they merely live together. The following year he married actress Sue MacManamy.

Like many legitimate actors of his day, Kruger looked upon movies as trash, and it was only the large salary offered by Cosmopolitan Productions—owned by William Randolph Hearst—that induced him to make *Under the Red Robe* (1920). He made other silent films in the East but without much enthusiasm for the medium. Otto was never a big star on Broadway or in pictures but in both media he had a solid reputation among producers and the public. He replaced George M. Cohan in *The Meanest Man in the World* in 1921, and when Noel Coward and Gertrude Lawrence in 1931 left their starring roles in *Private Lives,* Otto stepped in opposite Madge Kennedy (widowed and living in Los Angeles). He was Paul Muni's replacement in the title role of *Counsellor-at-Law* in 1932.

Harry Cohn, the head of Columbia Pictures, brought Kruger to Hollywood for the first time in 1933, but when he arrived Cohn couldn't decide what to do with him. When M-G-M bid fifty dollars a week higher for his services, Otto went with the Culver City lot, a loss that Cohn admittedly regretted for years. His first talkie was *Turn Back the Clock* (1933) with Mae Clarke (single and living in North Hollywood). It was followed by sixty-eight oth-

176

ers. Among them were *Springtime for Henry* (1934) with Heather Angel, *Dracula's Daughter* (1936), *Exposed* (1938) with Glenda Farrell (living in Manhattan), *Dr. Erlich's Magic Bullet* (1940), *Hitler's Children* (1943) with Tim Holt ** and Bonita Granville (married to multimillionaire Jack Wrather and living in Beverly Hills), *Wonder Man* (1945) with Virginia Mayo (married to Michael O'Shea and living in the San Fernando Valley), *High Noon* (1952), *The Young Philadelphians* (1959), and, his last, *Sex and the Single Girl* (1964).

Between film assignments Otto returned to Broadway for such plays as *The Moon Is Down* (1952) with the late William Eythe. The greatest disappointment of his professional life was when he was unable to come to New York in *Advise and Consent* in 1960. He had played the role of the president of the United States during the tryouts to excellent notices, but suffered a stroke and could no longer remember the lines. His second stroke came after his last film, and he informed his agent that he was no longer available for work in any medium.

During World War II Otto worked as a food coordinator in the Los Angeles County Agriculture Department. After his retirement he tackled gardening, orchid raising in particular, with enthusiasm and knowledge. His time now is divided between his flowers and the television set in his Bel Air home.

He and Sue have a daughter and several granddaughters. Of the few people from the film colony the Krugers see these days is their old close friend Robert Young.

With Mrs. Kruger on the lawn of their Bel Air, California, home. *Clifford May*

A Paramount publicity still, 1926.

LOUISE BROOKS

The immortal of the motion-picture screen was born in Cherryvale, Kansas, in 1906. Her father was an attorney. When she was fifteen years old her pianist mother enrolled her at the famous Denishawn Dance Studios in New York City. She toured for two years with the late Ruth St. Denis and Ted Shawn and then joined the chorus of the *George White Scandals of 1924*, with Dolores Costello ** and the late Dorothy Sebastian. That fall she left *Scandals* to dance at the Café de Paris in London. In 1925 she returned to Broadway to work for Flo Ziegfeld in *Louie the 14th* and the *Ziegfeld Follies*. Late that year she signed a five-year contract with Paramount Pictures. For two years Louise worked at their New York studios until they closed and moved to the Hollywood lot. Paramount used her often but never to any advantage. In all, she played a bit part in *The Street of Forgotten Men* (1925), went into *The American Venus* (1926) which starred Esther Ralston,** *A Social Celebrity* (1926) with Chester Conklin,* *It's the Old Army Game* (1926) with W. C. Fields, *The Show-Off* (1926) with Lois Wilson (unmarried and living around the corner from United Nations headquarters in Manhattan), *Just Another Blonde* (1926) with Dorothy Mackail (who lives at the Royal Hawaiian Hotel in Honolulu), *Beggars of Life* (1928) with Richard Arlen,* and *The Canary Murder Case* (1929) with William Powell ** and Jean Arthur (who lives with a lady companion in total seclusion in Carmel, California).

In October 1928 her option was up for renewal. Sound had come ⅳ the movies and Hollywood was in a state of panic. Paramount cut salaries, and studio head B. P. Schulberg told Louise she could continue at the weekly seven hundred fifty dollars she had been getting but without the $250 increase her renewal called for. But Louise accepted an offer from the great German director G. W. Pabst. Together they made the masterpiece *Pandora's Box* (1929), which is still shown throughout the world as an example of the silent film at its very best. Pabst also starred her in *The Diary of a*

178

Lost Girl (1929), which created a great stir because of its sordidness. Even the censors who criticized it acknowledged its great artistry. Louise left for France and made *Beauty Prize* (1924), highly praised by film buffs even today.

When she returned to New York, Paramount ordered her to report for work on the sound version of *The Canary Murder Case* (1929). She refused. Instead, the voice of Margaret Livingston, the widow of Paul Whiteman (she lives in retirement in Bucks County, Pennsylvania) was dubbed in for the remake. Meanwhile, Paramount let it be known that Louise Brooks had failed in talkies because her voice was unsuitable. Actually, it is doubtful that any producer would have touched her because of Hollywood's unwritten law never to hire stars who are litigants against you and/or refuse to do a picture, whether justified or not.

The girl whose bangs inspired the comic strip *Dixie Dugan* continued to make a film now and then, but the parts were humiliatingly small and few. Fatty Arbuckle directed her in *Windy Riley Goes Hollywood* (1931) and director Norman Foster used her in *It Pays to Advertise* (1931). After that she made *God's Gift to Women* (1931) with Laura La Plante.** From 1933 to 1935 she was with the ballroom dancer Dario at the Persian Room of the Hotel Plaza in Manhattan. Following that she made *Empty Saddles* (1936) and *Overland Stage Raiders* (1938). Harry Cohn talked her into dancing in the corps de ballet for the Grace Moore movie *When You're in Love* (1937) in exchange for a screen test.

In the early forties Louise worked in radio for a few years in New York City, doing soap operas, and then she spent two years in a publicity office followed by two years as a salesgirl on the seventh floor of Saks Fifth Avenue. "Then I became more or less a bum until I was rescued by a famous millionaire friend who has given me a small monthly allowance ever since—God bless him!" In 1956 she moved to Rochester to do research at the Eastman House film collection for a book she plans to write, which seems to be a career in itself. Many of Louise's articles on motion pictures have been in movie magazines both in the United States and abroad.

In retirement in Rochester.

A top leading man in 1929.

JOHNNY MACK BROWN

The handsome leading man of the silents and Western hero of talkies was born in Dothan, Alabama, in 1904. He attended public schools in Alabama and then went to Alabama University where he became a top football player. His school went to the Rose Bowl in 1926, but the team was less than happy. Their opponent, the University of Washington, was top rated and Alabama University was not taken very seriously. Johnny was eager to see California, where the game would be played, and was more optimistic about its outcome—it was his catching a fifty-nine-yard pass that beat Washington 20 to 19 on New Year's Day, 1926.

That same year Johnny married his college sweetheart, Cornelia Foster. After graduation that spring, he coached the freshman team. He left after being contacted by George Fawcett, a talent scout who had seen him play in the Rose Bowl. He was taken to Hollywood and offered tests by several major studios. Johnny signed with the newly formed Metro-Goldwyn-Mayer for five years. His debut was with Claire Windsor ** in *The Bugle Call* which also starred Jackie Coogan. That year Marion Davies chose him for her leading man for the *Fair Co-Ed*.

Before his change of image Johnny played opposite Greta Garbo in three vehicles: *Divine Woman* (1928), *The Single Standard* (1929) with Nils Asther (who lives in Stockholm, Sweden), and *Woman of Affairs* (1929). He was with Joan Crawford in her first big hit, *Our Dancing Daughters* (1928). Mary Pickford had Johnny opposite her in her first talkie, *Coquette* (1929), for which she received an Academy Award. Johnny also costarred with Eleanor Boardman (now Mrs. E. d'Arrast, completely retired and living in Santa Barbara) in *The Great Meadow* (1931).

But it was a film that preceded that one that would change his image. In

1930 King Vidor directed Johnny in a classic sound version of *Billy the Kid,* made in a 70-mm process called Grandeur Screen. It was a huge success and is often screened today by cinema societies throughout the world. Johnny Brown was a splendid rider, and handsome, and his southern drawl worked perfectly. He made over two hundred pictures after *Billy,* nearly all Westerns. Including non-Westerns, some were *Son of a Sailor* (1933) with Joe E. Brown,** *Three on a Honeymoon* (1934) with Sally Eilers, *It Ain't No Sin* (1934) with Mae West, *Valley of the Lawless* (1936), *Wells Fargo* (1937), *Bad Man from Red Butte* (1940), *Ride 'Em Cowboy* (1942) with Bud Abbott ** and the late Lou Costello, *Land of the Lawless* (1947), *Stampede* with Rod Cameron and Gale Storm (both are residents of Encino, California. Miss Storm is married to an insurance broker), and *Colorado Ambush* (1951).

Johnny made most of his features at Universal and Monogram once he left M-G-M in the early thirties. In the late forties, as realist Western heroes became the trend, he found fewer and fewer parts. His four children married and left the big Beverly Hills mansion, in which the family had lived so extravagantly, and Johnny sold it. He and Mrs. Brown moved into a Park La Brea apartment, a middle-class community in Los Angeles, where they live today. In 1961 and 1962 Johnny was the maître d' of The Tail of the Cock restaurant in Los Angeles. He admitted to the press that although he enjoyed meeting people and seeing old friends, he kept the job only because he needed the income. He has been seen on such television shows as *Perry Mason* and *Wells Fargo.* A. C. Lyles, a producer of low-budget Westerns at Paramount, has used Johnny in several of his pictures these last years, for which Johnny is "very grateful because I know damn well that he doesn't need me, and I sure can use the money, but how big can a role be for a fat old man like me?"

Alongside a proclamation making him a member of the Football Hall of Fame.
Diana Keyt

In her 1921 triumph, *The Queen of Sheba*.

BETTY BLYTHE

The superstar of early silents was born Elizabeth Blythe Slaughter on Hope Street in Los Angeles on Labor Day 1903. "And I've hoped and labored ever since," she said once. Her father, a lawyer, died when she was two years old. Her uncle was the writer Samuel G. Blythe. She and her two sisters were brought up by their mother. She was a great tomboy and quite a good baseball player. She said recently that she was into her twenties before it ever occurred to her that she might some day marry.

Her mother encouraged her to pursue a career on the stage and even provided voice lessons. Betty was in her early teens when she went to Europe with a theatrical company to play in *The Peacock Princess*. Shortly after her return to the United States, her mother died, and Betty was faced with making her own way in the world. She appeared on Broadway in 1915 in a play called *High Jinks* and went on the road the following year with the hit *So Long Letty*.

When the tour ended, Betty was living in a girls' club on West Seventy-third Street in Manhattan with seventy dollars owed in back rent. One of the girls felt sorry for her because she seemed so depressed, and, offering to pay Betty's carfare, invited her to an interview she had at the Vitagraph Company in Brooklyn. Betty was sitting in the reception room waiting for her friend when the director W. P. S. Earl and his star Earl Williams noticed her. She was hired on the spot.

Her most important vehicles were *The Queen of Sheba* (1921), with Betty in the title role wearing nothing above the waist but delicate, artistically arranged chains *She* (1917), later remade as a talkie with Helen Gahagan Douglas,* and *Chu-Chin-Chow* (1925). Some of her other efforts were *Over the Top* (1918), *Miss Ambition* (1918) with Corinne Griffith,**

The Silver Horde (1920), *Charge It* (1921), and *In Hollywood with Potash and Perlmutter* (1924).

By the time talkies came in, Betty was reduced to playing much smaller roles. She became part of the sound era but though her voice was no obstacle, her career did not pick up. Her parts were not very large nor were the pictures particularly good, but she did work fairly steadily. She was seen in *Pilgrimage* (1933), *The Perfect Clue* (1935) with David Manners,* and *Sis Hopkins* (1941) with Judy Canova.*

Most of her income during and following this period was derived from acting and diction lessons, which she gave in her large home in Hollywood. Occasionally she would appear with a road tour in such plays as *The Man Who Came to Dinner* (1940), and *Wallflower* (1944).

Her husband of thirty-four years, Paul Scardon, died in 1954. In 1967 Betty sold her house and moved into the Motion Picture Country House in Woodland Hills, California. She was there only briefly when it was announced she would wed a seventy-four-year-old former studio translator. The marriage never took place.

Also living at the Country House at the time was Nell Craig, who played Vashti in Betty's *The Queen of Sheba*. "She was always a perfect devil to work with," said Betty, "and after all those years she still refused to speak to me. But I must admit that she was a splendid Vashti." Betty recalls the film well. One story she tells at the slightest encouragement is about the time she tested for it and tripped over the elaborate train, ripping the gown nearly in two.

As one of the few name Country House residents, Betty is very popular among the former movie people who now make it their home. Oldtimers are spellbound by her tales of the old Hollywood Hotel dances where she made merry with her friends Charles Ray, William Ince, and Elinor Glyn, all now deceased. Betty's cottage was once occupied by the late Gareth Hughes who had costarred with her in two pictures.

Relaxing in the Motion Picture Country House library. *Michael Knowles*

In 1939, when he signed with NBC to produce television programs.

MAX GORDON

The producer of some of Broadway's best-remembered plays was born Michael Salpeter on June 28, 1892, in New York City. Until his early teens, his family lived in a tenement on the Lower East Side. At that time his father's income as a tailor was supplemented by the salary of his older brother, who had taken the name Cliff Gordon and become a top comic monologist on the burlesque circuit.

Cliff got his younger brother a job as advance man for burlesque shows traveling throughout the East. After his brother's sudden death in 1913, Max began to produce one-act plays for vaudeville. His first success, *Straight,* came only after failing on the first couple of tries. Then he teamed with Al Lewis and together they produced *Welcome Stranger* (1920), *Rain* (1922), *Easy Come, Easy Go* (1925), and *The Jazz-Singer* (1925) with George Jessel. The partnership was dissolved after the last hit, which had been directed by Lewis who continued in this capacity in the theatre. Max took a high-salaried job with a vaudeville chain, booking their top acts until the 1929 stock crash both wiped out a major portion of his savings and all but brought show business to a standstill.

In 1930, mortgaging the few securities he had left and borrowing from everyone he could, Gordon presented the memorable *Three's a Crowd* which starred the late Clifton Webb, Libby Holman,* and Fred Allen. It was the first in a string of hits that lasted right into the fifties. But his most impressive period was during the Great Depression when he not only raised money at a time when it was almost impossible but also produced some highly sophisticated theatre.

Part of his success lies in his unblemished reputation for complete honesty, not only in financial dealings but personal as well. He presented Noel Coward and the Lunts in *Design for Living* (1932–1933) on a handshake with star-writer-director Coward. The best artists in the business began to

184

come to him to produce their works. Another element in his enviable career is his never being a writer or performer. Gordon, unlike so many producers, had never wished to be anything but what he was on opening nights—a member of the audience. There was none of the envy that is basic to many producers. He liked his people and they liked him. The audiences began to respond to marquees stating Max Gordon Presents as a guarantee of quality, taste, and imagination.

Of his many hits, probably the best remembered are *The Band Wagon* (1931) with Fred and Adele Astaire,* *The Cat and the Fiddle* (1931), *The Farmer Takes a Wife* (1934), *Jubilee* (1935), *Othello* (1937), *Junior Miss* (1941), *Over Twenty-One* (1944), *Born Yesterday* (1946), *The Late George Apley* (1947), and *The Solid Gold Cadillac* (1953). During the 1933–1934 season he had four hits running at one time: *Roberta, Her Master's Voice, The Shining Hour,* and *Dodsworth.* Gordon's last effort was the ill-fated *Everybody Loves Me* in 1956.

His two ventures into motion picture production were *Abraham Lincoln in Illinois* (1939) and *The Actress* (1953). A production advisor to NBC Television as early as 1939, he produced the *Frank Sinatra Show* on television during the 1951 season. In 1963 he and Lewis Funke wrote his autobiography, *Max Gordon Presents,* a straightforward book about his years as a Broadway giant.

Max Gordon has been married since 1921 to the former Mildred Bartlett, who had appeared in vaudeville and silent films as Raye Dean. The Gordons have no children and are often seen at opening nights. Although no longer active in the theatre, he is still a familiar face at theatrical parties and along Broadway where he maintains an office, which he visits almost daily. Here he freely advises younger showmen and chats with old friends. About his only interest aside from the theatre and his wife is the racetrack, which he visits several times a week during the season.

In his office recently. *Diana Keyt*

At Paramount, 1929.

SALLY BLANE

The leading lady known best for being Loretta Young's sister was born Elizabeth Jane Young in Salida, Colorado. Her mother had to get off a train so that she could be born. In 1915, when Sally was five years old, Mrs. Young separated from her husband and took the family of five to Hollywood. Eventually all of the Young children worked as extras, although Sally was the first to get featured parts. Her first extra work came when the late Ben Alexander's mother took him home from location when food there became scarce: Sally got the part as a sea nymph in *Sirens of the Sea* (1917), which starred Jack Mulhall (now living in Hollywood).

When she was fourteen, director Wesley Ruggles spotted her dancing at the Café Montmarte and asked her to test for the part of Dorothy Gulliver's friend in the *Collegian* series. She got the role and shortly afterward signed a contract with Paramount. At the same time her younger sister Loretta signed with First National. Sally's first big part for the studio was in *Rolled Stockings* (1927). Even after Sally had become a leading lady, she remembers bumming a ride on many occasions from an extra named Dennis O'Keefe because her mother, who had a strong influence on her children's professional and personal lives, would not allow her to buy a car.

Sally then made such films as *Horseman of the Plains* (1928) with Tom Mix, *Vagabond Lover* (1929) with Rudy Vallee, and *Little Accident* (1930) with Anita Page (Mrs. Herschel A. House of Coronado, California). She then went to work for such low-budget studios as Chesterfield and Artclass. She appeared in *Trick for Trick* (1933) and *No More Women* (1934) with Edmund Lowe (an invalid at the Motion Picture Country House). There was also a series of B pictures in the midthirties with Frankie Darrow (residing with his wife in a hotel on Hollywood Boulevard).

In 1937 Sally married the director and former actor, Norman Foster, on whom she had had a crush ever since he had dated Loretta a few years before. In 1935 Sally had gone to England to work for a year where she and Foster remet at a dinner party given by Colleen Moore.** She worked occasionally until 1948 when one of her children became ill just as she was scheduled to do a television show. It was then that she decided she would devote all her time to her family.

During World War II the Fosters lived in Mexico where her husband made Spanish-language pictures.

Sally says of her career and the inevitable comparison people made of her with Loretta Young: "She had more drive than the rest of us. Loretta was always really ambitious. She would turn down parts that I would have given anything to have played, but she never realized how much I wanted them. But while Loretta was concentrating on her career, I had all the beaus." Asked about her own ambitions she said, "There were two things against me. I was never resilient enough. I've always felt rejection deeply and took it personally. Then, too, I wasn't as slim as Loretta. The director Dorothy Arzner [retired and living in Palm Springs, California] once said I had the body of a peasant." The part she most wanted was played by Helen Vinson (married to a wealthy and socially prominent Manhattanite) in *I Am a Fugitive from a Chain Gang* (1932). Mrs. Paul Muni had vetoed Sally and she was cast instead in a lesser part.

The Fosters live on Foothill Drive in Beverly Hills. They have a son in college and a daughter who is a photographer. Her other two sisters and one brother had brief careers in films also. Pollyanne, the eldest, is married to a businessman. Georgianna, the youngest, is married to Ricardo Montalban, and Jack is an attorney and the father of five.

Asked if she would do it all over again Sally said, "No, I think I'd try for the stage. I never felt I was photogenic. People ask if I watch my old movies on television. I don't. I never liked a single thing I did."

Now Mrs. Norman Foster, in her Beverly Hills home. *Clifford May*

Under contract to Universal Pictures, 1940.

BILLY HALOP

The better-looking Dead End Kid was born in Brooklyn in 1921. His mother had been a professional dancer when she married Billy's father, a lawyer for Trunz Meat Packing. The family moved to Long Island, where Billy and his sister, Florence, who became an actress, were brought up. From the time Billy was six years old he worked steadily. He played the title role on radio's early serial *Bobby Benson of the B-Bar-B*, in which his sister played Polly Armstead. He also did the radio show *Skippy*, which had been a popular book and movie, and at twelve played Romeo in a radio production of *Romeo and Juliet*, after adding Puck in *A Midsummer Night's Dream* to his repertoire. He worked with Maude Adams in a number of radio dramas and was a regular on radio's *The March of Time*. Some of Billy's best training came from the late Nila Mack, whose *Let's Pretend*, the famous all-kiddie award-winning show, paid $3.50 per performance. He is still in touch with "The Lady Next Door" (Madge Tucker, now retired and living in Connecticut), who hosted the junior-acted story time show. By the time he was seventeen, Billy was making $750 per week though he got only $10 for an allowance, the rest being invested for him by his parents. Along with his radio work, he appeared with the Ringling Brothers Circus and traveled for a while with a rodeo.

Billy's big break was his appearance on Broadway in *Dead End* (1935), followed in 1937 by an excellent screen version, but today those old days are anathema to him. He never got on well with most of the boys and had a particular, and reciprocal, dislike for the late Leo Gorcey. They were the most popular of the team, and from the beginning vied for top billing and salary.

In 1939 Billy asked Jack Warner for the raise his contract called for, from a weekly one thousand dollars to twelve hundred dollars. Warner stalled and Billy went to Universal where he tried without success to become a star in his own right and thus shed the Dead End image. He made a few hard tries with such pictures as *Tom Brown's School Days* (1940) with Freddie Bartholomew * and *Mob Town* (1941) with Anne Gwynne (now Mrs. Max Gilford of Beverly Hills) and Dick Foran (retired in Van Nuys, California). Later, after dozens of feature films and mountains of publicity and a stint in the Coast Guard, in 1945 he was still considered by casting directors one of the Dead End Kids. He refused to play juvenile delinquents, toured United States Army bases in Europe with *Golden Boy,* and worked again in radio, but the image was still there—and remains today.

In 1954 Billy was arrested on a drunk charge; it was followed by a suicide threat, and a nervous breakdown. Then his wife contracted multiple sclerosis, and has been an invalid ever since. Billy stopped drinking and devoted most of his time to taking care of her in their Pacific Palisades home. He became interested in the techniques of geriatrics-trained nurses who worked with her, and today he is a registered nurse specializing in such cases. By the time he gets them, most of his patients are so sick they don't notice that it is the former Dead End Kid who is attending them. He takes only private cases and is in constant demand. To add to his troubles, Billy has had two coronaries but continues to smoke.

Billy Halop has by no means given up acting but turns down offers for television commercials. He will work only in the conventional media. The best his agent has been able to offer was a bit part as a waiter in the Dick Van Dyke starrer *Fitzwilly* (1967). But he is still typed and it grates on him: A young casting director asked him what he had done, and he walked out of the office in a rage. He is particularly bitter about those who have been his friends when he was in a position to help them: he says he worked with actor Chuck Connors nonstop for several days to coach him for an audition that made him a star. Now Billy says he is lucky to get a "hello" from him.

Halop, whose memory of his career seems somewhat more impressive than the record shows, says, "I've been a star on stage, in radio, and in movies. I'll be one again."

The only reminder of his Dead End days is his longtime friendship with a fellow Dead End Kid Gabe Dell, whose career has prospered lately on Broadway.

At home recently in Pacific Palisades, California. *Clifford May*

Typical Donnelly, 1945.

RUTH DONNELLY

The wise-cracking character actress and comedienne was born in Trenton, New Jersey, in 1896. Her father was a newspaper editor, music critic, and columnist. Ruth made her professional debut in the chorus of a touring production of *The Quaker Girl* (1913), followed with a comic role in *Maggie Pepper* the same year, and then toured in *Under Cover*.

She was first seen on Broadway in *A Scrap of Paper* (1914) as a telephone operator. The legendary George M. Cohan spotted her flair for comedy and from 1914 to 1917 used her constantly in his productions. She attributes much of her success to his sponsorship and guidance. She was again a switchboard operator in *Going UP* (1917), which was followed by *A Prince There Was* (1918). In 1920 she played Ethel Nutt in *As You Were* and Kitty Crockett in *The Meanest Man in the World*. Aggie was her character in *Madeline and the Movies* in 1922.

After the stock-market crash of 1929 Broadway productions were rare, with little more work available in a dying vaudeville. On the advice of friends Ruth came to Hollywood where to her surprise she landed a job almost immediately, in *Blessed Event* (1932) which starred Mary Brian (now Mrs. Tomasini of North Hollywood, California) and Lee Tracy (who retired from acting since a cancer operation left him speechless, though he now communicates through a mechanical larynx). Ruth signed with Warner Bros., a studio noted for keeping its salaried players working. She was put into one film after another, some good, some bad. Regardless, she was good in every one, usually portraying a friend, secretary, or landlady to the star. She soon acquired the reputation she had earned on Broadway—that of a scene stealer. Her jibes and side-glances were the delight of studio and theatre audiences. Such pictures as *Footlight Parade* (1933), *Wonder Bar* (1934), *Mr. Deeds Goes to Town* (1936), and *A Slight Case of Murder* (1938) established her as one of the top funny women of the movies. Her sharp lines were delivered with expert timing and aplomb, and her gemlike performances often brought short bursts of applause, even from matinee

190

audiences who seldom knew her name. Ruth was often confused with Winnie Lightner (the widow of director Roy Del Ruth now lives in Van Nuys, California), who retired in the midthirties.

Ruth also appeared in *Mr. Smith Goes to Washington* (1939), *My Little Chickadee* (1940), *This Is the Army* (1943), *The Bells of St. Mary's* (1945), and *Cinderella Jones* (1946). She feels that her best Hollywood work more often than not ended on the cutting-room floor. In *The Bells of St. Mary's* she danced an Irish jig, as Sister Michael, which everyone found delightful, but when the final print was exhibited the scene was gone. *Photoplay* gave her a gold medal for her performance, or what there was left of it. "They want you to be good, but not too good. Marie Dressler told me about the heartbreaks she had, and I thought of her words often as I looked in vain for a bit or a scene that took years of experience," she says. Ruth worked steadily until the late fifties in such features as *The Snake Pit* (1948), *The Spoilers* (1955), *and Autumn Leaves* (1956).

In 1958 her husband Basil de Guichard, an executive with an airplane company, died. They had been married since 1932. Not caring much for the atmosphere in Hollywood, Ruth moved to Manhattan.

Although she does not consider herself retired, she has worked very little since. She would do a play if the part suited her but she refuses to go on the road. In 1963 she was seen on Broadway in *The Riot Act*.

Ruth lives in a residential hotel for women on East Fifty-seventh Street, where she is recognized daily by fans. "None of them bothers me," she says. "In fact I hope no one ever walks by without saying hello." Ruth reads a great deal of Mary Baker Eddy, is very interested in astronomy, and works on her autobiography, which she will call "Tripping Along." Asked why she did not do television commercials, she replied: "I'm not ending a career of over fifty years selling soap."

Guesting with television host Joe Franklin. *Gary Leavitt*

The child star at seven.

DICKIE MOORE

The cute little boy from the 1930s movies was born in Los Angeles in 1925 of French-Irish parentage. According to Dick, as he is now known, a family friend—then secretary to Fox Picture's President Joe Schenk—had to be picked up at Dickie's house one day when her car stalled, and the studio's casting director came to get her. Dick who was playing in his crib, was seen by the director who thought he bore a close resemblance, at eighteen months, to John Barrymore. That was the beginning of his career. "Frankly," he admits, "it just sounds too pat to be completely true." Whatever the facts, Dick made his screen debut playing Barrymore as a baby in *The Beloved Rogue* (1926). But his earliest recollections are of making *Passion Flower* (1930) with the late Kay Francis and *Squaw Man* (1931).

Contrary to what most people think, adult actors, Dick claims, were always very nice to him. He has unpleasant memories only of a few directors and teachers who tutored him at studio schools. Although he was allowed to see his films, he had little interest in them and felt no personal ambition until his late teens. In his early adolescence he was quite withdrawn and self-conscious and in his acting then he could not bring himself to exhibit any of the charm or cuteness he had projected so strongly as a little boy. He says: "I knew what was wanted of me and I knew how to do it,but I resented those qualities very much and simply couldn't bring myself to do it anymore." Later he became very interested in his art, and after a stint in the army during World War II covering United States Pacific operations for *Stars and Stripes,* the army newspaper, even acted in, co-directed, and co-produced a two-reel 35 mm short subject called *The Boy and the Eagle,* which was nominated for an Academy Award in 1949.

Of his over two hundred and fifty films he is probably best remembered for *Blonde Venus* (1932) in which he played Marlene Dietrich's little boy, *Ol-*

iver Twist (1933), *Peter Ibbetson* (1935) with Ann Harding (retired and living in Westport, Connecticut), *Sergeant York* (1941) with Gary Cooper, and *Miss Annie Rooney* (1942) opposite Shirley Temple.

He was very displeased with the latter part of his career with his roles in *Dangerous Years* (1947) and *Killer Shark* (1950). However, he finished strong in *Member of the Wedding* (1952), his last picture. In 1956 he was on Broadway with Siobhan McKenna in George Bernard Shaw's *Saint Joan,* but such parts were infrequent. He was working steadily but as a featured player on such television shows as *Captain Video,* which starred Al Hodge (now an executive with Olsten's Temporary Personnel, Inc., in Manhattan) in the title role.

In 1957 Dick accepted the newly created post of public relations director of Actors Equity. He worked closely for seven years with his good friend, then Equity's president, Ralph Bellamy and Lois Wilson then on the executive board and with whom he had made some of his early pictures. Dick left in 1964 to form his own public relations firm, Dick Moore Associates. It has prospered as a producer of industrial shows. Actor Don Koll, who has worked for him on several occasions, called him "the most considerate producer I've ever encountered."

Dick no longer minds being kidded about "Dickie" and his former image: "There was a time when I bridled whenever a fan bothered me for an autograph or someone started with the jokes about dimples but now I'm rather pleased that someone remembers. Since my two boys no longer watch my *Our Gang* pictures on television, it's nice to know that someone is impressed," he said. Dick and his family live on Manhattan's West End Avenue.

A public relations executive now.
Diana Keyt

As Peter Pan in the movie released by Paramount in 1924.

BETTY BRONSON

The elfin actress of the silent screen was born Elizabeth Ada Bronson in 1907 in Trenton, New Jersey. When she was three years old, her family moved to California where she attended Catholic schools. She studied dancing under Michael Fokine and played bit parts in such films as the one in which she debuted, Alice Brady's starrer *Anna Ascends* (1922). Soon after, Sir James Barrie chose her for the title role in the screen version of his fantasy *Peter Pan* (1925). Barrie, who first met Betty two years after the picture was made when she visited him in London, had picked her over some of the top stars of the day. He had wanted a girl who would not immediately be identifiable as a star or remembered for other roles. Her performance in the classic confirmed his judgment.

Betty Bronson overnight became a serious rival to Mary Pickford. In fact, after the release of *Kiss for Cinderella* (1926) it was thought for a time that she would eclipse America's Sweetheart. Praise for her charm and ability was almost unanimous.

Betty suffered the fate of most stars catapulted to fame and popularity on one or two great successes. She was never able to equal, much less top, them. Paramount tried to change her image. Betty says they tried to protect her with the proper vehicles but she was unable to retain the huge popularity she enjoyed briefly. She had a small part in *Ben Hur* (1926) and played opposite Ricardo Cortez ** in *Not So Long Ago* (1925). The late Adolph Menjou and Florence Vidor were her costars in *Are Parents People?* (1925). Her other credits include *Ritzy* (1927) with the late Gary Cooper, *The Singing Fool* (1928) with Al Jolson (whom she found "extremely difficult"), and

194

The Medicine Man (1930), Jack Benny's screen debut. Her oddly pitched voice was no asset in sound movies. One of her last was *The Locked Door* (1930) with the late Rod La Rocque. In 1932 Betty married Ludwig Lauerhaus, a bond specialist. They spent their honeymoon at San Simeon and then moved to Asheville, North Carolina, where she wrote a column, *Peeping Pixie,* for the local paper. In 1937 Betty attempted a comeback when she played the romantic interest in the Gene Autry starrer *The Yodelin' Kid from Pine Ridge.* After that it was retirement for Betty Bronson.

Betty lives with her retired husband in Altadena, California. Her only son, born in 1935, teaches at the University of California. She sees none of her former movie associates, mostly because she was younger than they and never became close. She is admittedly anxious to work again. Her last appearance was in the Lana Turner–Dean Martin film *Who's Got the Action?* (1962), and she has done television segments on *Dr. Kildare* and *My Three Sons.*

Betty Bronson's appeal went beyond that of an actress. Her gamine quality induced many crushes, which still endure. The New York *Post* columnist-critic Richard Watts often refers to her as one of the romantic inspirations of his younger years, and at a more recent meeting for lunch still found her "charming and delightful."

Film buffs were relieved when Eastman House unearthed a print of *Peter Pan* after it was feared none existed. When it was shown at the Museum of Modern Art, in New York, in 1969, Betty, who had flown in for the occasion, received a tremendous ovation. Film historian William K. Everson considers her one of the silent screen's "greats."

As Mrs. Ludwig Lauerhas, Altadena, California. *Marion Parson*

Wallace and Senator Taylor
with son, Gregory, at the Progressive party convention, Philadelphia, July 1948. *UPI*

SENATOR GLEN H. TAYLOR

The country's first show-business politician was born in Portland, Oregon, in 1904. His father, a minister and an activist in Democratic politics, had been the youngest Texas Ranger in history. Glen, the twelfth in a family of thirteen children, was a sheepherder in the Bitterroot Mountains before he went to work for his brother Ferris managing a silent-movie house. In 1921 he joined Ferris's newly formed drama-stock company and traveled throughout the West. In 1931 Glen formed his own drama company, the Glendora Players, and married actress Dora Marie Pike. When they failed to get bookings, Glen changed the name to the Glendora Ranch Gang and thereafter billed himself as the "Crooning Cowboy." As they moved about the United States during the depression, Taylor became increasingly aware of poverty everywhere. He had always read a great deal, in his spare time, and now he became very interested in economics. The late Dr. Francis E. Townsend's popular Townsend Plan (1933) fascinated him. It called for an old-age pension supported by Federal tax funds. "Then the thoughts I'd been having for some time began to prey on my mind," he said recently. "I knew that what I had read made perfect sense. We had an abundance of everything here in the United States. It was only a matter of educating the people to what could be done. The object of all knowledge being action, I decided to run for office."

In 1935 he tried unsuccessfully to organize a farm-labor party in the Nevada and Montana mountains and in 1937 lost the Democratic primary for a House seat. In his bid for Congress, he had done a bit better than expected, campaigning in his performing Western gear, but still he could not beat the nominee of the Democratic machine. In the Idaho Senate seat race in 1938, he won the primary, but when the Democratic county chairman resigned and threw his support to the G.O.P. candidate, Glen was buried at the polls in the general election. Glen ran again in 1940 and again captured the nomination in the primary. Still the Democratic machine was opposed, and refused to give him any money for his forthcoming campaign. But he ran anyway.

After his third try, Glen had to resort to a job in a California war plant as a painter's helper just to support his family. In preparation for his next campaign on his return, Taylor and his wife wrote over three thousand hand-written letters to former supporters in past elections. This time, in 1944, he won the primary *and* the general election, much to the chagrin of the local politicos. His first Senate speech was an endorsement of Henry Wallace as secretary of commerce, and in the all-night session held to fight the Taft-Hartley Bill he spoke for eight hours and twenty minutes. Glen was an early and enthusiastic supporter of the United Nations and riled many in the administration with constant references to "the militarists in the war and state departments."

When Henry Wallace asked Taylor to run as his vice-president on the Progressive party ticket in 1948, he gave it long and hard thought. He knew that they couldn't possibly win, that he could never be reelected if he left the Democratic party, and that unlike Wallace he was not rich and would have no money to fall back on once his Senate term expired. Still, he decided to run "because I knew it was the right thing to do. There were things that had to be said and neither Truman nor Dewey were saying them," he said recently, adding, "Looking back on it all I'm glad I did. We only won 1,156,000 votes but we drove Truman from right of center way over to the liberal side."

During Taylor's successful Senate race he wore a toupee, which he made himself, and believes it helped him win the election. Once out of office, he began to manufacture his "Taylor Topper." The company, with offices in all major United States cities and in London as well, is headquartered in Millbrae, California, where Glen and his wife reside. He has done much better financially than he could have as a senator, or perhaps a vice-president.

The former senator, referred to by contemporaries as "real Taylor ham," by no means is disinterested in local or national politics. He can hardly bring himself to comment on Ronald Reagan, whose very name makes him shudder. In California's 1968 presidential primary, Taylor voted for Eugene McCarthy.

Today, wearing one of his own "toppers," to which he credits his 1944 seat.

A Fox featured player, 1934.

PEGGY FEARS

The show girl and chanteuse was born in New Orleans in 1906. Her father, who had a credit-clearing house, took the family to live in Dallas when Peggy was still a child. While in her teens she married against her family's wishes but agreed to an anullment if she could go to New York. She left Dallas soon after. In New York, millionaire Jock Whitney took her to the Club Richman, where on a dare she sang a chorus with Harry Richman.* Some of the Whitney party were chorus girls and they suggested Peggy audition later that week for the *Ziegfeld Follies*. She already had a small role in *Louie the 14th* (1925), which starred Leon Errol, but she was more impressed with the *Follies*. On the day of the audition the first girl to be chosen from the line-up was the famed beauty Anastasia Reilly (married and living in Palm Beach, Florida). Peggy was picked also but did not remain a Ziegfeld Girl long: the star, Vivienne Segal, came down with a very bad throat and Peggy was to be her replacement. Vivienne Segal became so angry that she refused to allow Peggy to wear her costumes. Fanny Brice and Ziegfeld intervened, and Vivienne and Peggy became such good friends that when in 1927 Peggy married Alfred C. Blumenthal, to whom she was introduced by Charlie Chaplin, Vivienne was her maid of honor.

Blumenthal was the mastermind behind some of movie magnate William Fox's biggest real estate deals and made a fortune in the process. Blumie, as Peggy called him, and his wife lived lavishly on a huge estate in Larchmont, New York, entertaining the top personalities of the day, including their close friend Mayor Jimmy Walker. Spending money was Peggy's favorite pastime. There were four Rolls Royces in the family and a charge account at Cartier's that carried two hundred and fifty thousand dollars on one ring alone.

198

Peggy began to produce her own plays but her only real hit was *Music in the Air* (1932). In 1933 she and Blumie separated, and Peggy later signed a movie contract with Fox films, announcing: "From now on, money is my god!" She immediately made *Lottery Lover* (1935), in which she received third billing and little notice. The year before, she had been on Broadway for a brief time in *A Divine Moment*. At one point she had a dress shop on Madison Avenue, but that went bankrupt. In 1938 she announced that she was pawning her jewels in order to eat and was available for nightclub work. A month later her mother killed herself by gas, and Peggy began a lengthy series of litigations against Blumie for back alimony, furniture, a Rolls Royce, and a bonus "for not bothering him." She claimed that if her demands were not met she might have to go on relief. In 1939 she received $44,801 of the $70,000 she was claiming from her ex-husband, who died broke in Mexico in 1957.

Peggy Fears was never a big name in clubs though she did have a following for some years. Unlike most entertainers, she liked nightclubs both as a performer and as a patron.

In 1955 she financed a new hotel and boat club at the Fire Island Pines. It was so successful that in 1959 gangsters offered to buy her out. She refused and the building was burned to the ground. She set to work the next day to have it rebuilt, this time in fireproof aluminum and in 1964 sold it at a handsome profit.

Peggy lives on Sunset Plaza Drive in Los Angeles with Tedi Thurman, the former Miss Monitor and fashion model she introduces as her niece. They have been living together for nearly twenty years. Peggy's health has greatly improved since she had a cancerous tumor removed from her leg several years ago. Also, her usual heavy alcohol intake has been greatly reduced since her doctors forbade her to drink anything but wine, which seems to have curtailed the public scenes she and Tedi Thurman had undergone at regular intervals at her former boat club.

At home on the Strip. *Richard Lamparski*

A Universal Pictures publicity portrait, 1931.

ELLIOTT NUGENT

The actor-director-playwright was born in Dover, Ohio, in 1900. His father was J. C. Nugent, a well-known actor and playwright, and his mother and sister, Ruth, were on the stage also. Elliott attended Ohio State University, where he began a lifetime friendship with James Thurber. Together they helped edit the college newspaper and years later they coauthored the smash Broadway play *The Male Animal* (1940).

Elliott made his stage debut in 1921 in the hit play *Dulcy*. The following year he and his father coauthored and acted in *Kempy* on Broadway, one of ten father-and-son collaborations on Broadway. Elliott also acted in the screen version, called *Wise Girls* (1930) and that same year played opposite Marion Davies in the *Dulcy* movie version, *Not So Dumb*. But his Hollywood debut had been in 1929 in *So This Is College* with his old friend Robert Montgomery.

Elliott appeared briefly in *Romance* (1930) and to this day he is asked about the star, Greta Garbo, whom he has never met. The following year, Jean Arthur was his leading lady in *Virtuous Husband* (1931). Nugent's last picture was *The Last Flight* (1931) with Richard Barthelmess and David Manners.*

By this time Nugent had become much more interested in directing plays and films. He now says that after his first picture was released he never expected to make it as a movie star: "I was very pleased with myself when they told me that several dozen fan letters had arrived addressed to me. Then I learned that Bob Montgomery was drawing several hundred."

In Hollywood he concentrated on directing, with some memorable results. Some of his efforts were *The Mouthpiece* (1932), *Life Begins* (1932) with Eric Linden, *Three Cornered Moon* (1933), *She Loves Me Not* (1934) with Bing Crosby and Eddie Nugent (no relation but an old friend, who now lives in Manhattan), and Miriam Hopkins (single and living in Beverly Hills), *Two Alone* (1934) with Tom Brown (living with his mother in

Sherman Oaks, California) and Harold Lloyd ** in *Professor Beware* (1938), and *Up in Arms* (1944) with Danny Kaye. He and producer Samuel Goldwyn quarreled over Kaye's leading lady in that one, but Nugent won and the newcomer he had nixed for the part became a star under the name Virginia Mayo.

In the meantime Nugent was one of Broadway's top leading men. His *Male Animal,* in which he also starred along with Leon Ames (owner of one of the country's largest Ford dealers, in Los Angeles) and Gene Tierney (married and living in Texas), was a smash on Broadway and was sold to the movies. He played opposite Katharine Hepburn in the highly civilized *Without Love* in 1942 and followed it the next year with one of the longest and most popular runs on record, *The Voice of the Turtle,* in which his costar was the late Margaret Sullavan.

Among his last works was the film he directed, *My Favorite Brunette* (1947), which starred Bob Hope; a co-producing role in the Broadway hit *The Seven Year Itch,* which starred Tom Ewell, who was replaced by Nugent during his vacation; and his direction of Broadway's *Greatest Man Alive* (1957), which starred Dennis King.

The last few years of Nugent's life have been clouded by mental illness and alcohol. In 1953 he was arrested for drunk driving in Los Angeles, and is frank about his many stays at the Institute for Living, a hospital in Hartford, Connecticut, for the mentally disturbed. There have been times when his health has improved sufficiently to get him considered for a directorial spot in a Broadway show, but then he lapses into his "manic-depressive cycles." During such periods, he has engaged in some outrageous behavior, public and private.

In 1964 his Hollywood novel *Of Cheat and Charmer* was published, and in 1968 he followed with his autobiography *Events Leading Up to the Comedy,* an extremely frank revelation of his life.

Nugent lives with his wife of over forty years, former actress Norma Lee, in a large, expensively furnished apartment on Manhattan's East Fifty-seventh Street.

As he appears today. *Werner J. Kuhn*

Under contract to Paramount Pictures, 1937.

MARY CARLISLE

The movie actress who epitomized the co-ed of the 1930s was born in Boston, Massachusetts, in 1912. When she was four years old her father died, and her mother brought her to Hollywood to live. Ten years later Mary and her mother were lunching in the Universal commissary when the studio production head, Carl Laemmle, Jr. (retired and living on Tower Road in Beverly Hills) spotted her and gave her a screen test. Complications arose because of her age, and it was decided that she would finish school before pursuing an acting career.

Mary had an uncle associated with M-G-M. One day she got a call to come to the studio in two days, prepared to dance. She spent most of the next forty-eight hours with a dance coach and arrived at the Culver City lot ready to begin her career. She was sixteen years old.

Mary's success in films did not come overnight. She frequently worked as a bit player before she began to catch on in the early thirties. In 1933 she was one of the Wampus Baby Stars but before she became a name she appeared in as many as eighteen movies in as many months. She was in *Night Court* (1932) with Anita Page, *Murder in the Private Car* (1934) with Charles Ruggles (who lives in poor health in Los Angeles), *It's in the Air* (1935) with Jack Benny, and *Tip-Off Girls* (1938) with Lloyd Nolan.

Mary is best remembered for the three pictures she made with Bing Crosby: *College Humor* (1933), in which he introduced the song "Down the Old Ox Road," *Double or Nothing* (1937), and *Dr. Rhythm* (1938) in which he sang to her "My Heart Is Taking Lessons."

Mary's mother became the second wife of the late steel millionaire Henry J. Kaiser, and her aunt—her mother's twin—was married to the late cameraman Alvin Wyckoff.

In 1934 Mary began dating James Blakeley, son of Mrs. Grace Hyde, a Park Avenue socialite. She and Blakeley, a flying supervisor, saw a great deal of each other until 1937, when Mary went to London for a while. Shortly afterward she announced her displeasure with the roles she had been given and stated that she simply did not want to play any more sweet, well-brought-up young college girls. Hollywood, however, was unable to see her any other way, and there were plenty of younger girls around to accept the parts Mary refused. Her swan song was with Richard Carlson (who lives in Sherman Oaks, California) in *Baby-Face Morgan* in 1942.

In 1942 Mary and Blakeley were married and she retired. She devoted all of her time during the next few years to running her Beverly Hills home and raising their one child, a son, who recently graduated from college. Her husband is an executive with Twentieth Century-Fox studios.

For the past nineteen years Mary Carlisle has been surprising her old fans when they come into the Elizabeth Arden Salon on Wilshire Boulevard in Beverly Hills where she is the manager and one of its best advertisements. Mary was hired and retained for her competence and charm rather than for any glamour she might add to the organization. Until her death in 1967, Elizabeth Arden, whose ego and unpleasant disposition were legend in the beauty business, refused to allow her employees to be publicized in any way. After she was gone, Mary was approached by a number of interviewers only to find that she had no wish whatever to talk about her days in the movies. She still sees many of those she worked with in the thirties, such as Bing Crosby, but refuses to discuss them or herself for publication.

At the Bistro Restaurant in Beverly Hills. *Jon Virzi*

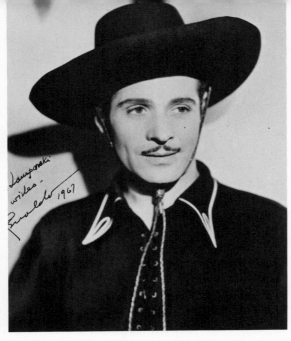

Riding high as the Cisco Kid, 1945.

DUNCAN RENALDO

The star of silents and early talkies known to television audiences as the Cisco Kid was born in Spain in 1904, and named Renaldo Duncan. He arrived in the United States in 1921 when the ship on which he was a seaman caught fire in port in Baltimore. While waiting for the vessel to be repaired Renaldo met a movie director who showed him the drawings for a set to be made of Havana's docks. Renaldo, who had sketched since childhood and whose ship had just left Cuba, informed him that the artist's renderings were incorrect. He offered to draw the set as it should be and was hired at fifteen dollars a week. When he wasn't designing sets at the studio, located on Manhattan's West Forty-fourth Street between Eighth and Ninth avenues, Duncan was chasing rats. He became interested in movies and talked himself into a part in *Bright Shawl* (1923), which starred William Powell,** Jetta Goudal (married to interior decorator Howard Grieve and living in Los Angeles), and the late Richard Barthelmess. After that Duncan appeared in the title role in a number of shorts on Beethoven, Schubert, and Schumann. He continued to act in films but was also assistant director, director, assistant producer, and writer as well. *Down to the Sea in Ships* (1923), which first brought attention to Clara Bow, had him as assistant director. The year before, he had traveled with his friend the late Robert Flaherty as his assistant on the famous Flaherty documentary, *Nanook of the North*.

Renaldo had a lead role in Thornton Wilder's *Bridge of San Luis Rey* (1929). He had been impressed with the book, could not interest a studio or producer, optioned the property, and finally sold it to Charles Brabin, the director-husband of Theda Bara, who sold it to Metro for fifty thousand dollars. Renaldo got five thousand and was promised the role. His performance

204

won him his role in the same studio's first talkie, *Trader Horn* (1931). M-G-M spent over three million dollars and shot 5.5 million feet of film throughout Africa to make the classic in which the only other white performers were the late Harry Carey and the beautiful Edwina Booth, who became very ill during the shooting. Although it is widely believed that she died shortly after the picture was made, she lives in Los Angeles and has worked at the Mormon Temple there since her illness.

After appearing in a host of B films, in 1943 he played Lieutenant Berrendo in *For Whom the Bell Tolls.* The Spanish actor is recognized constantly by young people who had him for a baby sitter when they watched him on television in the *Cisco Kid* series. He played in 164 of the movie features and 156 half-hour television shows and was producer on quite a few of them. His sidekick in most of them was the late Leo Carillo. The name of his horse in the series was Diablo. A number of identical horses were used in the role and several are still with Duncan today. One is twenty-seven years old.

The *Cisco Kid* series is still in television around the world, but the last episode was filmed in 1956. The last picture Duncan appeared in was *Satan's Cradle* (1949). He and his wife, a nonprofessional, live on their Rancho Mi Amigo in Santa Barbara, California, where he is a director of the town's Old Spanish Days Fiesta. His daughter, Stephanie, is a music teacher and his boys, Jeremy and Richard, are in college. Duncan's close friends are cameramen Billy Bitzer and Leon Shamroy and actor Pat O'Brien. A great deal of his time is spent in Cisco Kid personal appearances in South America, Australia, and Canada where he is still a big draw. He has been working for some time on paintings from sketches he did on his sixteen-thousand-mile trip across Africa during the filming of *Trader Horn.*

In mufti today. *Shifra Haran*

Dangerous and intriguing in the late twenties.

EVELYN BRENT

The leading lady of the silent screen was born Mary Elizabeth Riggs in 1899 in Tampa, Florida. Her mother, still in her teens, died shortly thereafter. During her childhood Evelyn lived in Brooklyn and Syracuse. Very soon she was on her own, and her first jobs were as a model. With the advent of World War I she was already appearing in movies. From 1915 to 1916 she was under contract to Popular Plays and Players, a producing company affiliated with Metro. After the armistice she went to England, where she was a chorus girl in *The Ruined Lady,* a West End production that opened in June 1920. While abroad she made over a dozen films, mostly in England, including two in Holland and one, *The Spanish Jade* (1922), in Spain. The last was her first success. On the strength of it she was brought back to Hollywood to costar with Douglas Fairbanks, Sr., in *The Thief of Bagdad* (1924) but at the last minute she was replaced. Instead, she was put into *Held to Answer* (1923), which was made at Metro and starred James Morrison (still a bachelor and living in retirement in Greenwich Village). During the filming she became ill and had to complete her scenes from a hospital bed. The same year she was named a Wampus Baby Star.

Evelyn worked a great deal during the twenties but none of her features enhanced her career or her public image. During 1923 and 1924 she appeared in seven pictures for Fox, all bad. Then she went to Film Booking Offices, where she made fourteen mediocre photoplays such as *Dangerous Flirt* (1924) and *Midnight Mollie* (1925).

In the midtwenties Evelyn signed with Paramount. The studio tried to change her image but didn't seem to know exactly what it wanted. In one film, *Love 'Em and Leave 'Em* (1926), she was veiled in mystery and weighted with clothes. Not until Josef von Sternberg directed her in the character Feathers McCoy in his masterpiece *Underworld* (1927), did she emerge

206

a star. A year later he used her to advantage again in *Drag Net*. Her part in his *The Last Command* (1928) was smaller but the picture was a huge success. The late Gary Cooper and William Powell ** were her leading men in *Beau Sabreur* (1928).

Then talkies took over the motion-picture business, but her voice, which was good, did not save her career. She made *The Silver Horde* (1930) with Louis Wolheim for RKO and produced her own starrer, *Pagan Lady* (1931), for Columbia. *Silver Horde* set no box-office records but *Pagan Lady* was an outright failure in spite of her popular leading man, Conrad Nagel.

By 1933 Evelyn was considered washed up in movies and had embarked on a vaudeville tour, which gave her a couple of years' work and her last husband, Harry Fox. She had been married before to Bernie Fineman, from 1922 to 1927, and to Harry Edwards following her divorce from Fineman. In 1935 she made *Home on the Range* with Jackie Coogan (now living in the San Fernando Valley) and Randolph Scott. Now and then Evelyn appeared in cheapies for studios like Chesterfield and Monogram. One of the last of her infrequent efforts was *The Golden Eye* in 1948.

After making over 125 feature films, the former star worked a while during the 1950s with the Thelma White Agency in Hollywood, where she represented actors. Lately, a cult of film buffs has enshrined her in a niche rivaling some of the superstars of her era.

Widowed since 1959, Evelyn shares a small apartment in Westwood Village, California, with her friend of forty years, Dorothy Herzog. Here she receives loyal fans from everywhere, many born well after her best films were made. Philosophical over the fact that her fortune is gone (she lives on a very small income) and that her canonization by fans has come too late, she replied recently to one fan, thanking him for his compliment and interest: ". . . but where were all you people when I needed you?"

Today in her Westwood Village apartment. *Diana Keyt*